Getting Beyond "Interesting"

Getting Beyond "Interesting"

Teaching Students the Vocabulary of Appeal to Discuss Their Reading

Olga M. Nesi

LIBRARIES UNLIMITED

AN IMPRINT OF ABC-CLIO, LLC
Santa Barbara, California • Denver, Colorado • Oxford, England

Library of Congress Cataloging-in-Publication Data

Nesi, Olga M.
    Getting beyond "interesting" : teaching students the vocabulary of appeal to discuss their reading / Olga M. Nesi.
        pages cm
    Includes bibliographical references and index.
    ISBN 978–1–59884–935–6 (pbk.) — ISBN 978–1–61069–225–0 (e-book) (print) 1. Reading (Middle school)—Activity programs. 2. Literature—Study and teaching (Middle school)—Activity programs. 3. School libraries—Activity programs. 4. Book talks. 5. Children—Books and reading. I. Title.
LB1632.N347   2012
428.4071′2—dc23   2012012353

ISBN: 978–1–59884–935–6
EISBN: 978–1–61069–225–0

16 15 14 13 12   1 2 3 4 5

This book is also available on the World Wide Web as an eBook.
Visit www.abc-clio.com for details.

Libraries Unlimited
An Imprint of ABC-CLIO, LLC

ABC-CLIO, LLC
130 Cremona Drive, P.O. Box 1911
Santa Barbara, California 93116-1911

This book is printed on acid-free paper ∞

Manufactured in the United States of America

For my mother—my first and best teacher ever.

Contents

CD-ROM Contents

(Please see the About This Book section for suggestions for how to use these.)

Appendix A Items:

A-1 The Book Hook

A-2 Proposal for Administration Worksheet

A-3 Reading Survey

A-4 Summary vs. Appeal Terms

Illustrations

Preface

In the best of all possible worlds, the development of personal reading preferences takes place organically, over a lifetime, and is advanced primarily by voracious and broad reading. If we are fortunate, we are raised in a print-rich environment, surrounded by adults who love to read and share this joy openly and ceaselessly with us from our earliest days. We are read to every day. We are taken to libraries and bookstores. We are encouraged to begin our own collections of books. Over time, we grow naturally into our reading lives. Somewhere along this path, if we continue to be motivated to read and if we are lucky indeed, we may discover the one special book that changes reading from a pastime into a compulsion. Upon discovering this book, we want desperately to find as many more like it as possible—to recreate the experience and the emotions and sensations of escaping into the world of that first most perfect book—the one the author surely wrote with only us in mind.

As a middle school librarian, a large part of what I do is help students find that one perfect book and then find as many more like it as possible. Indeed, the goal of all good readers' advisory is to do just that: extend for readers the experience of their last great read. Like any trained school librarian, I turned to the tools of the readers' advisory trade: print and electronic "what to read next" resources. Beyond these, I relied far too heavily on genre- and subject heading-driven recommendations—despite being fully aware of the fact that not all books of one genre "feel" the same when they are read. Nor are books on a common subject necessarily written the same. Would you ever recommend Bram Stoker's *Dracula* to a child who just read and loved *Twilight* by Stephenie Meyer? Probably not—despite the fact that both books are about vampires.

Beyond this, I assumed fully the burden of being telepathically able to predict what my students might enjoy reading . . . and therein lay the flaw. Without the expectations that students would take ownership of their particular reading preferences and learn how to verbalize them intelligently, I was largely doomed to doing a lot of "near-miss" readers' advisory, punctuated by the occasional purely accidental hit. A critical piece was missing: appeal terms.

In search of direction, I turned to Professor Mary K. Chelton—cofounder of VOYA and my mentor from the Queens College Graduate School of Library and Information Studies. She suggested I familiarize myself with Joyce Saricks's writing on articulating appeal in Readers' Advisory Service in the Public Library (ALA 2005). There I learned that while subject headings describe the actual content of a book, appeal terms are adjectives that can effectively convey readers' reactions to the elements of a book (Saricks 2005, 65). Using appeal terms to describe the story elements of pace, characterization, storyline, frame/tone, and style "frees us from reliance on plot summaries" (Saricks 2005, 64) and, further, allows us to connect seemingly disparate titles to each other by determining their common appeal. Most importantly, however, is the idea that these adjectives help readers precisely define the reading experience they are looking for. Thus, the idea of systematically teaching our students appeal terms was born. By utilizing a specially designed form (The Book Hook), our students would be taught how to distill the essence of the books they had read so that they might share their reading experiences with their peers (rather than only with their teachers in the form of summary-based book reports).

About This Book

As the idea of teaching appeal terms and Book Hook writing veers from more traditional approaches to teaching literature, the book starts with a suggested implementation plan. The governing presupposition here is that since the school librarian may not be able to reach the entire student population on a consistent basis, collaboration with English Language Arts teachers will be critical. Even in schools with smaller student populations, the more collaboration with other teachers in the building, the more successful the endeavor will be.

A Book Hook and Appeal Terms section follows the implementation plan. The "meat" of the book is in the lesson ideas, forms, and resources for teaching both Book Hook writing and appeal terms concepts to middle and high school students. All these materials are primarily meant to spark reflective practice. After all, what works in one school with one particular set of students may need to be changed to work with another class in the same school and may need substantial modifications to work in yet another school altogether.

About the CD-Rom Contents

A very deliberate decision was made to include a number of items on a CD-ROM for use with this book. The materials chosen for inclusion on the CD-Rom are those that you are encouraged to manipulate to suit your needs (Appendix A items) and resources that should facilitate the process of teaching appeal terms and Book Hook writing to your students (Appendix B items). Some suggestions for specific uses follow.

Appendix A Items (A-1 to A-10)

Most of these items can loosely be thought of as forms/black line masters or workshop materials. They are included on the CD-Rom to facilitate both editing (which you are strongly encouraged to do) and printing. Static versions of all of these are also available in the book in Appendix A.

Appendix B Items

B-5: Excel Spreadsheet of Picture Books (With Appeal Terms)

B-6: Excel Spreadsheet of Short Story Book Hooks (With Appeal Terms)—Only available on CD-Rom

B-7: Excel Spreadsheet of Book Hooks for Novels (With Appeal Terms)—Only available on CD-ROM

The reason for including Excel versions of several of the resources on the CD-Rom is to give you the ability to sort the spreadsheets in a number of different ways to suit your particular needs. The most useful sort for these documents will be by appeal term, as it will enable you to quickly determine what resources you can use to teach particular appeal terms.

B-7: Book Hooks Without Covers Alphabetical by Title

Use the contents of this Word document to start a Book Hook binder in your library. This document provides a ready-to-use batch of Book Hooks sorted alphabetically by title. Choose the ones you like, replace the Book Hook image with book cover images, print in color, hole punch, and place in a Book Hook binder. Add your own Book Hooks as you read out of your library's collection.

B-10: Appeal Terms Glossary

This glossary is included on the CD-ROM so that you can add definitions and synonyms (and their definitions) to expand the book discussion vocabulary of your students.

Acknowledgments

First and foremost, thanks to Mary K. Chelton for pointing me in the direction of Joyce Saricks's work on appeal terms and for firmly prodding me to write this book and then supporting me throughout the process of doing so. I am grateful for your mentorship and guidance.

Thanks to those who gave permission for me to incorporate their work into mine: Joyce Saricks (for the use of appeal terms), Fiona Creed (for the use of her whimsical drawing on the Book Hook), Barbara Stripling and all the Summer 2010 Appeal Terms Workshop attendees (for the *Winston the Book Wolf* Book Hooks), and Kyra Blair (for the Reading Survey). Thanks also to Hachette Book Group and Little Brown and Company (for granting permission for the use of book jacket images for *The Mysterious Benedict Society* and *Maximum Ride—Angel Experiment*).

Thanks to the Language Arts Department at I.S. 281 Joseph B. Cavallaro in Brooklyn, New York, for incorporating appeal terms and Book Hook teaching into already overflowing curricula. You are the best colleagues a school librarian could ever ask for.

Thanks to the Too Numerous to Name Individually, who contributed to all parts of the process, including Rena Deutsch ("This is too much for an article. You're going to have to write a book."), friends far and wide who cheered me on, and all my students for bringing profound joy to my life.

Thanks to editors Sharon Coatney and Emma Bailey of Libraries Unlimited for believing in this book and for helping to make it a reality. Thanks also to those involved in the process of producing an attractive final printed product.

Many, many thanks to my far better half Frank for his unwavering encouragement and support. You are my Gibraltar.

Part One

A Plan for Implementing the Teaching of Appeal Terms and Book Hooks

- Making the Case for Teaching Appeal Terms Concepts
- Making the Case for Teaching Book Hook Writing
- A Proposal for Administration
- Appeal Terms Workshop Activities for the English Language Arts Department
- Book Hook Workshop Activities for the English Language Arts Department

Making the Case for Teaching Appeal Terms Concepts

The overarching goal of all education is to create independent, life-long learners. Any endeavor that advances this goal is a worthy one to undertake. One would be hard pressed to find anyone in education who would openly deny the importance of reading fluency and the extent to which it is critical to overall academic achievement. We are largely in agreement on the following: There is no such thing as an academic subject that does not require reading fluency. It is also safe to say that the correlation between avid independent reading and reading fluency has been well established (and makes perfect sense). Not at all surprisingly, it turns out reading is much like any other skill—proficiency can only be achieved through practice. The more students read, the better they read; the better they read, the more they enjoy it; the more they enjoy it, the more they read. Before you know it, they are reading without being prompted to do so and a lifelong reading habit is born.

If Only It Were So Easy . . .

The chasm between reluctant reading and avid independent reading is both hair raising and undeniable. Yet part of the school librarian's everyday work is to find ways to move children gradually across the vertiginous drop. This is no small task and one that requires a variety of tools, endless patience, and constant work. Beyond this, it requires the cooperation and direct participation of the children themselves. Let's not fool ourselves here. Attempting to get across the chasm with an inert subject is both ill advised and guaranteed to be unsuccessful. Our students must build *with us* the bridge that will help them travel from one side to the other. Obviously, this "bridge" is constructed out of books. More specifically, it is built with books the child actually enjoyed reading. After all, they are the ones that best close the distance between reluctant and avid reading. We experience our greatest successes any time "perfect" books find their way into the mix and the child makes great strides forward toward wanting to read more.

You Don't Want To Make Any Sudden Moves Around Reluctant Readers . . .

Finding the "perfect" book for a reluctant reader without the student's own participation in the process is pointless at best and catastrophic at worst. This is the place where the ham-handedness of genre-driven readers' advisory sends our charges lurching back to the safety of their stance of reluctance. By way of providing an example: A student comes into the library looking for a book to read. I ask what she last read that she liked. She names a realistic fiction title. I hand her another realistic fiction title. Done. But of course, not all realistic fiction "feels" the same because books create unique experiences and emotional responses in readers. So maybe she was looking for realistic fiction with a humorous tone and I handed her realistic fiction with an edgy tone. I miss the boat with this child and she has a disappointing reading experience. If she is already an avid reader, it matters far less than if she is a reluctant reader. That's because the avid reader has already traversed the chasm. She will not stop reading simply because she did not enjoy this one book. If, however, she is a reluctant reader, the exchange is ripe for losing ground. The book she just finished reading is the first book she really loved. She is looking for a similar "read" almost as confirmation that this whole reading thing everyone goes on about so is actually as worthwhile as they say. The misstep of giving this child the wrong book is far greater because her tendency will be to revert to not reading.

While We're At It, Subject Headings Aren't Much Help Either . . .

Imagine if you will, that you and I are engaged in a readers' advisory exchange. You are the librarian and I am the patron. I come to you for a reading recommendation. When you ask me what I last read that I liked, I tell you: *Stiff: The Curious Lives of Human Cadavers* by Mary Roach. Would you deduce from our exchange that I was looking for more books on cadavers? Hopefully not, and that's because as a librarian and a seasoned reader, you understand that the subject matter of a book is but one of many factors that readers may find appealing. In the case of *Stiff*, in fact, you could probably safely assume the appeal wasn't about the subject at all, but rather about the way the book is written. In our exchange, you might next coax out of me what else I have read and liked (*The Art of Eating* by MFK Fisher, *Low Life* by Luc Sante, *An Anthropologist on Mars* by Oliver Sachs). With further prompting, you might get me to verbalize what, specifically, connects all the books together: an astonishing facility with language, a strong underlying wit, a fine eye for the absurd. Fortunately for you, I know what I like to read and how to express my likes and dislikes, and armed with this knowledge, you might now be able to recommend I read Joseph Mitchell, David Sedaris, or Florence King. In any event, you wouldn't send me off to read a *Gray's Anatomy* text. Readers' advisory with middle school students (even those who like to read) is a distinctly different experience because they are not able to verbalize what, precisely, appeals to them about a book they have just read and enjoyed.

. . . and Plot Summaries Are the Kiss of Death.

"First there's this boy . . . and then he . . . and then . . . and then . . . and then . . . and then . . . " While there is no denying that the events of a plot might well contribute to the appeal of a book, relying on plot summary to do readers' advisory virtually guarantees disappointment. To state the obvious: The point of readers' advisory is not to find the identical plot line for a patron, but rather to connect him or her with a similar reading experience. In fact, it is probably safe to say that if it were even possible to find multiple identical plot lines, reading the same "story" over and over again might quickly become tedious to a reader. In the end, it's about *how* the author conveys the events of the plot that either intrigues or dismays a reader. Drawing this out of students is an especially daunting task without the help of appeal terms. So, when a middle school patron is asked what he liked about Gary Paulsen's *Hatchet* (S&S, 1987), he immediately reverts to plot summary: "It's about a boy with a hatchet and he's lost in the wild and he uses the hatchet to survive." And while this is, undeniably what *Hatchet* is *about*, it does not at all help me know what the child enjoyed about the book. The actual exchange follows.

Me:	"Are you telling me you are looking for another book about a boy stranded in the wild with a hatchet?"
Student:	"Not necessarily."
To Myself:	Phew!
Me:	"O.K., so, what did you like about this particular story?"
Student:	"Well, it's interesting."
To Myself:	Oh no! Not the dreaded "interesting."
Me:	"What's interesting about it?"
Student:	"That he figures out stuff to do to survive."
Me:	"What else did you like?"
Student:	"It's exciting."
Me:	"What's exciting about it?"
Student:	"It has a lot of action because he faces danger."
Me:	"How did you feel when he was in danger?"
Student:	"It was suspenseful because I didn't know if he would survive or not."

Me:	"Did you like anything else?"
Student:	"I felt like I got to know the boy and how he was thinking when he figured out the stuff to do to survive. I wondered if I could do it too."

Were this child fully taught how to use appeal terms to describe what he liked about the book, our exchange might go something like this:

Student:	"I just read *Hatchet* and loved it. Is there something else like it?"
Me:	"What did you like about it?"
Student:	"That the story is action packed, the tone is suspenseful, and most of all, that I felt like I got to know exactly how the main character thinks to figure out problems."

Now, rather than automatically offering him another survival story (which may or may not meet his criteria for an enjoyable book), I can offer him Shane Peacock's historical fiction mystery *The Eye of the Crow* (Tundra, 2007) because it is also exciting and suspenseful and lets the reader into the mind of the protagonist, in this case, the young Sherlock Holmes. The advantage of the child reading across genres is a tremendous bonus here. He might not ever have considered it on his own and might have read a number of disappointing survival stories on the erroneous assumption that they are the only books that deliver excitement, suspense, and a glimpse into a character's thought process.

In a Nutshell

The reasons to teach appeal terms concepts are:

- Students learn to identify precisely what they like (and don't like) to read, thereby taking ownership of their reading. By encouraging them to take on this active role, we acknowledge and validate their personal preferences.
- The clearer they are about what they like (and don't like), the easier it is to help them find similar books to read to keep them reading and increasing fluency.
- Broader reading occurs as students venture across genres in search of a particular reading experience. This cross-genre reading opens up new reading worlds for our students.
- Aside from the established Vocabulary of Appeal (Figure 1), students are encouraged to use both synonyms and a wide range of phrases to express the "feel" of any given book they have read and liked. In this way, vocabulary is increased.

Making the Case for Teaching Book Hook Writing

What is a Book Hook?

Neither a summary nor a review, a Book Hook is a two- to three-paragraph distillation of the reading experience provided by a book. It starts from the reader's

From the list below, determine which appeal terms to teach your students.

Pacing
breakneck, compelling, deliberate, densely written, easy, engrossing, fast paced, leisurely paced, measured, relaxed, stately, unhurried

Characterization
detailed, distant, dramatic, eccentric, evocative, faithful, familiar, intriguing secondary (characters), introspective, lifelike, multiple points of view, quirky, realistic, recognizable, series (characters), vivid, well developed, well drawn

Story Line
action oriented, character centered, complex, domestic, episodic, explicit violence, family centered, folksy, gentle, inspirational, issue oriented, layered, literary references, multiple plotlines, mystical, mythic, open ended, plot centered, plot twists, racy, resolved ending, rich and famous, romp, sexually explicit, steamy, strong language, thought-provoking, tragic

Frame and Tone
bittersweet, bleak, contemporary, darker (tone), detailed setting, details of [insert an area of specialized knowledge or skill], edgy, evocative, exotic, foreboding, gritty, hard edged, heartwarming, historical details, humorous, lush, magical, melodramatic, menacing, mystical, nightmare (tone), nostalgic, philosophical, political, psychological, romantic, rural, sensual, small town, stark, suspenseful, timeless, upbeat, urban

Style
austere, candid, classic, colorful, complex, concise, conversational, direct, dramatic, elaborate, elegant, extravagant, flamboyant, frank, graceful, homespun, jargon, metaphorical, natural, ornate, poetic, polished, prosaic, restrained, seemly, showy, simple, sophisticated, stark, thoughtful, unaffected, unembellished, unpretentious, unusual

Source: Joyce G. Saricks, *Readers' Advisory Service in the Public Library,* 3rd ed. (Chicago: ALA Editions, 2005), 66.

Figure 1.   The Vocabulary of Appeal

personal point of engagement. That is to say: In order to write a Book Hook, a student will first need to be able to verbalize what "hooked" her. Even in books with broad appeal, Book Hooks will differ from each other, as each reader may be hooked by a different element of the story as developed specifically by the author. By way of example: Four students read Suzanne Collins' *The Hunger Games* (Scholastic Press, 2009). The first student is hooked by the pace at which the story unfolds. The second student may be hooked by the character development. The third may be hooked by the book's action-driven story line and the fourth by the darkness of the book's tone. The uniqueness of readers' experiences of this particular book should be reflected in their individual Book Hooks.

Tying up this personal distillation of their experience of the book is a fine thread of summary carefully woven throughout the Book Hook. Without giving away too much (and without reverting to trying to retell the entire story), students learn to select for summary only that which will give Book Hook readers a tantalizing glimpse into the story. Here too, the student's unique experience of the book should be in evidence. Thus, the student who was hooked by the dark tone of the story may choose to briefly

GET HOOKED ON READING!!	**GET HOOKED ON READING!!**

Title: _____

Author: _____

Genre: _____

Here's the Hook:

_____

_____

_____

_____

_____

_____

_____

_____

_____

_____

Three words or phrases that best describe this book are:

_____

_____

_____

Name: _____

Class: _____

Title: _____

Author: _____

Genre: _____

Here's the Hook:

_____

_____

_____

_____

_____

_____

_____

_____

_____

_____

Three words or phrases that best describe this book are:

_____

_____

_____

Name: _____

Class: _____

Figure 2.   The Book Hook (Artwork: Fiona Creed).

summarize bits and pieces of the plot that convey that darkness, while the student who was hooked by the pace will include for summary that which contributed to conveying the feel of the pace of the novel.

What should not be missed in all of this is the extent to which the writing of Book Hooks requires students to be emotionally as well as cognitively engaged with their reading. The best-written Book Hooks are those that offer such clear evidence of this reading engagement as to convince readers of the Book Hook to want to have the same reading experience by reading the book themselves. Unlike book reports (which tend toward interminable summary), Book Hooks have more in common with the kind of persuasive writing that characterizes book blurbs. The need to be convincing in the confines of a limited amount of physical writing space makes good Book Hooks challenging to write. Deciding what to leave out of a Book Hook becomes just as important as deciding what to include. Determining the most appropriate "emotional focus" for the Book Hook is central to the task, as is an overall familiarity with the concept of appeal.

Finally, the student is asked to provide a "snapshot" of the book in the form of three words or phrases. Here, students incorporate appeal terms to leave readers of the Book Hook with as clear a picture as possible of the book's broadest appeal. In this way, regardless of what personally hooked *them*, students learn to describe (*for others*) the potential appeal of each of the elements of the story. (See Figure 2 for examples of a Book Hook)

Sharing Book Hooks

Book Hooks = Sharing Reading Systematically

It is not at all by accident that the above section ends with the implied suggestion that Book Hooks are written by students for *others* to read. In fact, the idea of teaching students how to write them was born out of a desire to find a way for students to systematically share their reading with a broader audience of their peers (versus an audience of one English Language Arts teacher). No matter how much I talk about reading, when students share their reading experiences with their friends, more of them read. The Book Hook is a way to tap into the power of systematically using these peer recommendations to encourage students to read. A tremendous added advantage is the positive impact this sharing has on the reading culture of a building. Fostering regular communication about reading establishes and reinforces the importance of reading in your building. Surely the benefits of a strong reading culture can never be underestimated.

A note of warning: Obviously, Book Hooks are easiest to write for books one has actually been hooked by. As such, it is not advisable to ask students to write Book Hooks for books they did not enjoy reading. Clearly personal preference is just that—personal—and ideally, students would be able to write Book Hooks for any book they read (on the assumption that books they did not enjoy might be perfect for someone else). Unfortunately, however, being able to do so requires a degree of sophistication often beyond the abilities of appropriately self-centered adolescents. Besides, if the primary purpose of the Book Hooks is to use them to get students to share pleasurable reading they have done, it is counterintuitive to force them to write about an unpleasant reading experience. Attaching a forced writing assignment to a bad reading experience is not productive.

Finally, the best way to encourage our students to read books and write Book Hooks is to read books and write Book Hooks ourselves. Being exemplary models of the behaviors we expect from our students is by far the most effective way to convince them of our commitment to the endeavor. If our goal is to get as many students as possible hooked on reading, we must be willing to do the work necessary to systematically share our reading with them, and we should not limit our reading and Book Hook writing to only those books that appeal to us personally. After all, if the goal is to win as many students over to reading as possible, then we should read broadly and learn to find the potential appeal of a wide variety of books, not only those we have personally enjoyed.

Sharing Is Not Always Caring (A Word or Two of Caution)

Children want very much to please adults and seek our approval consistently (despite what may on occasion be viewed as evidence to the contrary). This is not power we should take lightly, especially when it comes to sharing reading experiences with our students. If we are pure in our intent to help children define and develop *their own* personal reading habits, then our actions should match this intent seamlessly. Students must be allowed to civilly disagree with us on particular reading recommendations we may have made. Our persuasive abilities are one thing; insisting that students like what we like is quite another.

Then there's the fact that even if we are not pressuring them to like what we like, because they want so much to please us, they may mistakenly assume the one sure-fire way to make us happy is to blindly agree with all our pronouncements. Nothing is quite as touching as students concerned that our feelings will be hurt if they did not enjoy a book we recommended. Teaching them how to intelligently verbalize what they disliked about a particular book is a golden opportunity for us to help them take complete ownership of their reading likes and dislikes. Part of what we teach them is that what makes us happy is not that they like exactly what we do, but rather that they are learning about themselves and their personal reading preferences and how to verbalize them. In the process, we set higher expectations for our charges when we require them to support their claims with some thought as to why they are making them. Thus, we help them further define precisely what they *do* enjoy: by a process of both accretion *and* subtraction. In the end, it is this respect for their personal preferences that most successfully encourages them to take true ownership of their reading. We should not do this work *for* them, but we need to be ever at the ready to assist them with it.

How Are Book Hooks Shared? Really, It's Best to Start Low Tech

Technology is a tool. When we forget this, it is at our own peril, and we end up being bullied by it in ways that are at best unnecessary and at worst endlessly frustrating (especially in the case of more advanced technologies). To clarify: The tool does not dictate the job. The job dictates the tool. We should not reach for the tool before knowing precisely *how* we will be using it and *what* we will be using it for. To clarify further: If you only had a hammer, but you did not need it to complete a particular task, would you create a "banging task" just so that you could use it? Probably not—because, clearly, you are not in search of creating more work for yourself, but rather in search of a tool to help you make the task you already have easier to accomplish.

In addition to the advantage of not creating more work for yourself, low-tech Book Hook sharing is the best way to start because it affords you the luxury of working out all the kinks specific to your environment and application. Once you and your colleagues have successfully piloted Book Hooks in your building, it becomes much easier to either create the technology that will best suit your sharing needs or (better yet) make an existing technology do exactly what you want it to do (versus the tool telling you what you have to do in order to use it). Obviously, the actual writing of the Book Hooks can (and should) be done utilizing word processing (if at all possible). If, however, computers are not available for even this part of the process, students may write the Book Hooks out by hand with the technology of pen or pencil.

Low Tech in the ELA Classroom

Three-inch ring binders with dividers for each student are set up in every ELA (English Language Arts) classroom. Each student's section houses his or her completed Book Hooks in plastic sheet protectors. The writing of Book Hooks is incorporated into each ELA teacher's class time as he or she sees fit. Ideally, the Book Hooks go through the same writing process (from drafting to editing to final draft) as all other writing that is done in the class. The primary difference is that once the student has written the final draft, it is housed in the binder. Then, during independent reading time, students in search of new books to read are encouraged to refer to the binder for classmates' recommendations.

If you are fortunate enough to be in a school with greater access to technology, you can next figure out how to house your school's Book Hooks in an online environment. The distinct advantage here is that everyone in the school has access to the Book Hooks of all classes (versus the scenario above in which students only have access to the Book Hooks of the classes taught by their particular ELA teacher). In either scenario, students are given a purpose for their writing and are directly engaged in creating a "reading product" in the form of a readers' advisory tool. The Book Hook binders of teachers fully vested in the endeavor are well utilized and a source of pride to the students who contribute Book Hooks to them.

Low Tech in the Library

In the library, Book Hooks can be shared in much the same way. Set up a three-ring binder for your own Book Hooks and start writing Book Hooks for the books you read out of your collection. Place the binder in an easily accessible spot, and encourage students to refer to it any time they are unsure of what they should read next. Set up a section within your Book Hook binder for Student Book Hooks and encourage students to contribute their best Book Hooks. Utilize a third section for any book lists you create and share over time. In this way, the binder becomes a one-stop readers' advisory tool for your library, specific to your school's reading experiences and your collection.

See Figures 3a and 3b for sample Library Book Hooks. (Note: Whenever possible, it is advisable that thumbnails of book jackets are used in the Book Hooks. Despite our insistence that books not be judged by their covers, cover images continue to be what entices us to pick a book up in the first place. If this is true for adults, it is true tenfold for our visually oriented students. In school libraries, including the book jackets for reading promotion is considered fair use and highly recommended.)

Low Tech Just Outside the Library—The Library Bulletin Board

An added advantage to writing your own Book Hooks and storing them in a library Book Hook binder is that they can be easily tapped for bulletin board material.

CAVALLARO IS HOOKED ON READING!!	CAVALLARO IS HOOKED ON READING!!
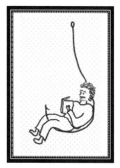	
Title: *Eye of the Crow—The Boy Sherlock Holmes. His 1st Case* **Author:** Shane Peacock **Genre:** Historical Fiction Mystery **Here's the Hook:** A beautiful young woman is found murdered in the back alley of a London slum in the year 1867. A young butcher's assistant is arrested for the crime and set to hang for it as well. Thirteen-year-old Sherlock Holmes knows the murder was committed by someone else entirely. Feel the thrill of sneaking with Sherlock into the homes of those he suspects of having committed the murder. Follow Sherlock into the dark, twisting, suffocating alleys of London as he solves his first case. **Three words or phrases that best describe this book are:** • Compelling pace • Suspenseful tone • Well-developed characters and setting **Name:** Miss Nesi (January 2009)	**Title:** *Remembering Raquel* **Author:** Vivian Vande Velde **Genre:** Realistic Fiction **Here's the Hook:** How did fourteen-year-old Raquel Falcone die? Was she accidentally or intentionally pushed in front of an oncoming car? Did she lose her footing and fall down under it? Or did she step in front of it on purpose? Told from the points of view of the people in her life, this quick read is full of small plot shifts and surprising plot twists, each packing a major emotional punch. **Three words or phrases that best describe this book are:** • Psychological tone • Multiple points of view in characterization • Engrossing pace **Name:** Miss Nesi (January 2009)

CAVALLARO IS HOOKED ON READING!!

Title: *The Seer of Shadows*

Author: Avi

Genre: Historical Fiction/Ghost Story

Here's the Hook:

The year is 1872, and fourteen-year-old Horace Carpentine is apprenticed to a photographer in New York City. Little does he know that he will soon discover a special talent he has for creating living ghosts through the process of taking and developing photographs. Join him on his spine-tingling, hair-raising adventures as he gives life once again to a dead, abused little girl named Eleanora. In this gripping tale of ghostly vengeance, the pages keep turning—nearly outside of your own power.

Three words or phrases that best describe this book are:
- Steady pace
- Spooky/foreboding tone
- Nail-biting suspense

Name: Miss Nesi (November 2008)

CAVALLARO IS HOOKED ON READING!!

Title: *Emma-Jean Lazarus Fell Out of a Tree*

Author: Lauren Tarshis

Genre: Realistic Fiction

Here's the Hook:

Seventh grader Emma-Jean Lazarus is extremely smart and also very strange (in all the best possible ways). Being smart and strange in middle school, however, is not exactly easy. None of her classmates understands how she thinks. Nor does she understand how they think. Full of quirky, well-developed, and extremely realistic and relatable middle school characters, this story is all about being true to oneself in the face of peer pressure and about finding ways to listen to one's own heart.

Three words or phrases that best describe this book are:
- Deliberate pace
- Heartwarming tone
- Gentle/character-centered story line

Name: Miss Nesi, (August 2010)

Figure 3a.   Sample Library Book Hooks Without Book Covers

CAVALLARO IS HOOKED ON READING!!

Title: *Maximum Ride—The Angel Experiment*

Author: James Patterson

Genre: Fantasy/Action Adventure

Here's the Hook:

With extremely short chapters, a fast pace, and a high-action story line, the pages of this book practically turn on their own.

Meet Max and her "flock"—six misfit kids who have been genetically mutated to be able to fly. Their escape from the lab is not being taken well by the scientists who created them. Enter the Erasers—other mutant kids designed to be tracking and fighting machines. Their only job now is to bring in Max and the flock . . . and every time Max thinks she is keeping the flock safe and out of danger, the Erasers show up out of nowhere.

Three words or phrases that best describe this book are:
- Extremely fast pace
- Action-driven story line
- Suspenseful tone

Name: Miss Nesi (January 2011)

CAVALLARO IS HOOKED ON READING!!

Title: *The Mysterious Benedict Society*

Author: Trenton Lee Stewart

Genre: Mystery

Here's the Hook:

Recruited for a most special and secretive mission, Reynie, Sticky, Constance, and Kate form the Mysterious Benedict Society. Near-constant suspense is created by riddles, puzzles, and a gradually unfolding mystery. A carefully crafted plot advances deliberately, with just the right amount of action and plot twists to keep readers engaged in the story line. What appears to be a resolved ending gives way to a cliff-hanger: The Mysterious Benedict Society is nowhere near done solving mysteries.

Three words or phrases that best describe this book are:
- Deliberate pace
- Suspenseful tone
- Well-developed characters

Name: Miss Nesi (June 2011)

Figure 3b.   Sample Library Book Hooks With Book Covers

Library Book Hooks Bulletin Board

Simply run off a quantity of Book Hooks you have written (with book jackets included and in color if possible), back them with bright paper, create a banner, and you're ready to go.

Low Tech in the Building

Once you are comfortable that Book Hook writing and appeal terms concepts have taken hold with your colleagues and students, set up a system for regularly culling student recommendations to develop a variety of suggested reading lists. Not all of these lists need incorporate the Book Hooks, but all should include appeal terms so that a wide range of reading preferences are addressed. For lists that do not include Book Hooks, refer students to the library catalog for brief plot descriptions to go along with the appeal terms. **(See B-1 - Student Appeal List in Appendix B for an example of this type of list.)** Do the same with your Book Hooks periodically, creating appeal terms–governed lists of Book Hooks for students to browse **(See B-2 and B-3 in Appendix B for examples of these lists.)** Be sure to keep copies of these in the library Book Hook binder as well.

Then Ramp the Technology Up . . .

Book Hooks themselves can be shared in any number of ways online. The flexibility afforded by many Web 2.0 environments at the very least guarantees that you will have options for wider Book Hook sharing. A good final goal to keep in mind is designing and populating a database of Book Hooks that will ultimately be searchable by single and/or multiple appeal terms simultaneously (so that, for example, students can find books with *both* a dark tone *and* a fast pace in one query). You may not arrive at this goal for some time, but keeping it well in mind will help you determine the salient details of the best low-tech paper structure to start out with. If you set all this up intelligently from the get-go, when the time comes for you to migrate into a Web 2.0 environment, you will be well prepared to do so with ease. Before selecting the best way for all this to happen for your school, carefully consider the following questions:

- Will you use an existing architecture such as Goodreads (www.goodreads.com/) or Shelfari (www.shelfari.com/) or will you create and/or customize your own?
- Will students post directly, or will someone preview what is posted?
- Will you need database and searching capabilities, or will you be satisfied with simple browsing?
- If the appeal terms appended to each Book Hook are thought of as tags, what tagging guidelines will you set up and how will you enforce them?
- What architecture (if any) will you set up to enable students to search by multiple appeal terms (or tags) simultaneously?
- How will the Book Hooks be accessed? Will they be open to the public, or do you prefer to set up a user name- and password-protected environment for your school's Book Hooks?
- What will you want this environment to look like? (That is, will an alphabetical list of titles with book covers hyperlink to the Book Hooks, or will appeal term tags hyperlink to them?)

Ironing out as many of the details as possible ahead of time will spare you headaches in the future and prevent you from having to repeatedly retrace your steps to work out each issue as it arises.

In a Nutshell

The reasons to teach Book Hook writing are:

- Students learn how to think about and verbalize what they enjoyed about a particular book.
- Students learn to write persuasively about positive reading experiences they have had.
- Students are given a clear purpose and audience for their writing. This audience extends well beyond their ELA teacher to include peers.
- In order to write good Book Hooks, students will need to be both emotionally and cognitively engaged with their reading. (Surely this will assist with comprehension.)
- Book Hooks offer a systematic way for students to share what they have read with their peers. As they read the Book Hooks of others, students learn about different perspectives and reading experiences (potentially of the same book).
- Book Hooks offer a systematic way for you to share with your students what you have read.

A Proposal for Administration

Assuming you are convinced that appeal terms and Book Hook writing make good sense for your building, you will next need to approach administration to get their support for the endeavor. Beyond making a case for adding these two elements to the ELA curriculum, you will need both an initial financial commitment (for the implementation of the low-tech sharing of Book Hooks) and ongoing administrative supervision of the project. Understand that while it is a given that you are the person that most promotes avid independent reading in your building, you cannot (and should not) be the only person to do so. Setting up a system for students and teachers to regularly share their reading experiences will advance the idea that the reading culture in your building is collaborative and strong.

It is more often than not the case that administrators are extremely busy. As such, it is best for you to be fully prepared in advance of actually asking for a meeting. Rather than expecting your administrators to read the parts of this book that would make your case for you, spend some time culling the more salient points from them. Be sure to add your own points to these so that when you do meet, you will be well prepared to make a coherent and well thought out case for your particular site. Use the **Proposal for Administration** graphic organizer **(A-2 in Appendix A)** to gather your thoughts in preparation for your meeting.

Here are some things that might help you to get administrative support:

- a well-thought-out explanation of precisely what you are suggesting the ELA department undertake and why
- a plan for professional development workshops for your ELA colleagues introducing both appeal terms and the writing of Book Hooks
- a plan and personal commitment to oversee the physical setup of classroom Book Hook binders for each of the buildings' ELA teachers
- a personal commitment to starting and maintaining a Book Hook binder in your library
- a personal commitment to providing the ELA department with the support and resources necessary to both begin and maintain the implementation of appeal terms and Book Hook writing

Workshops for the English Language Arts Department

Once you have successfully gotten administrative support for teaching appeal terms and Book Hook writing, you will need to get your colleagues on board. The reason for this is that without the commitment of the ELA department, these new concepts will not ever become fully ingrained in your students. While you will surely be involved in the rollout and may even teach a number of lessons to a number of classes, your ELA colleagues will be the primary teachers of this new material. As they see their students every day, they will also be the ones to continue reinforcing the appeal terms concepts and Book Hook writing skills.

A good way to get the ELA Department to consent to the changes you are proposing is to design and deliver two engaging workshops for your ELA teachers: one on appeal terms and one on Book Hook writing. Wherever possible, throughout the workshops, you will want to elicit from your colleagues their ideas about how to best go about making these proposed changes, since they are the ones that will most directly be impacted by what you are suggesting. Ask them how you can work together to implement these changes.

As you move through each of the workshops, you may in fact discover that your colleagues are already doing some version of what is being suggested. Persuasive writing is already taught by ELA teachers, and discussions about reading and writing are regular occurrences in the ELA classroom, as are conversations about the importance of independent reading. Where appeal terms are concerned, while ELA teachers probably do not teach all the specific terms identified by Joyce Saricks, they certainly do teach story elements in some detail. An added advantage here is that as teachers of English (and more than likely avid readers themselves), there is an excellent chance they will immediately recognize and understand the potential usefulness of the appeal terms concepts.

Helping people see what they are already doing that fits in with what you are proposing is a good way to make the change seem less dramatic. In the end, the more your colleagues contribute to the conversation of change and the best ways to implement it, the more vested they will be in making it work for their students and, ultimately, the school.

Because cookie cutter workshops are rarely effective, the workshops you ultimately design should be specific to your particular audience and needs. Time constraints will be another factor to consider. In the pages that follow, you will find a list of suggested appeal terms and Book Hook activities you may want to cover in your workshops. Where appropriate, materials are provided or suggested. Cherry pick those materials and activities you feel will best suit your needs and time constraints. Create additional material as you see fit. Make this process your own!

A Very Important Note:

A number of the activities suggested for the professional workshops will also be useful in teaching the students about appeal terms and Book Hook writing and will therefore be referred to again later in this book in the sections on teaching appeal terms concepts and Book Hook writing to students.

Appeal Terms Workshop Activities for the English Language Arts Department

The activities for the Appeal Terms Workshop are divided into three categories: Introductory, Middle, and Closing. A number of possible activities are suggested for each section of the workshop.

Introductory Appeal Terms Activities

1. The Vocabulary of Appeal
2. What Should I Read Next?
3. The Reading Survey
4. Summary vs. Appeal Terms

Middle Appeal Terms Activities

1. Whole-Group-Appeal Terms
2. Appeal Terms Carousel

Closing Appeal Terms Activities

1. Sorting and/or Collapsing the Vocabulary of Appeal

2. Broadening the Vocabulary of Appeal
3. Selecting Appeal Terms to Teach

Introductory Appeal Terms Activities

1. The Vocabulary of Appeal
2. What Should I Read Next?
3. The Reading Survey
4. Summary vs. Appeal Terms

This is the part of the workshop during which attendees are introduced to the concept of appeal terms being a well-thought-out vocabulary that helps readers define and describe precisely what they are looking for in a reading experience. As such, the activities are primarily centered on the vocabulary and why it is useful. Depending on how much time you will have for the workshop, try one (or several) of the introductory activities below:

1. Give out the list of appeal terms (**Figure 1 The Vocabulary of Appeal on page 5**) and generate a conversation with ELA teachers about how many of these terms they already address with their students and how they do so.
2. Ask attendees to complete the activity **What Should I Read Next? (B-4 in Appendix B).** If you prefer, create a list of books you have read (rather than using the one provided in form B-4). Discuss.
3. Ask attendees to complete the **Reading Survey (A-3 in Appendix A)** and discuss.
4. Ask attendees to complete the **Summary vs. Appeal Terms** activity **(A-4 in Appendix A)** and discuss.

Middle Appeal Terms Activities

1. Whole-Group-Appeal Terms
2. Appeal Terms Carousel

The body of the workshop is where you will want the attendees to internalize the concept of appeal terms introduced previously. The best way for people to do this is to read, assign appeal terms, and then discuss with others their choices of terms. As such, the activities in this section will require you to procure reading materials for teachers to work with. Obviously, you will not be able to read full-length novels in your workshop. Thankfully, it will not be necessary for you to figure out how to do so. It turns out picture books and short stories lend themselves extremely well to appeal terms activities due to their brevity. They have all of the same story elements as novels (namely: pace, story line, characterization, and tone), but get to the point much faster than novels do. As such, they are perfect for demonstrating much of the appeal terms vocabulary. In fact, where picture books are concerned, the illustrations provide an additional element of appeal (albeit clearly not one centered in language). To the extent that the illustrations are generally inseparable from the text, they can be used to deepen the teaching of the appeal concepts. Before beginning this activity, discuss the following with your attendees: In the very best picture books, the illustrations dovetail seamlessly with the text and enhance the appeal of the story elements. Not only do they help tell the story, they also contribute greatly to the feel of the book. Readers expect the illustrations in picture books to go with the text and augment the reading experience. When they do not, the picture book reading experience is either incomplete or jarring. In the end, this is what makes them such excellent tools to teach appeal terms concepts: the best of them visually illustrate appeal. Thus, readers would expect a story with a leisurely pace and gentle story line to be illustrated very differently than one with a compelling pace and a mythic story line—and a picture book with a humorous tone would look quite different than one with a bittersweet tone. (More on this later in Part II of this book, in the section on teaching appeal terms to students using the visual arts. Suffice it to say here that you do not want to ask your colleagues to ignore the illustrations, but, rather, to consider if and how they amplify the appeal of the story elements.) For the two activities suggested in this section, use the **Appeal Terms Worksheet (A-5 in Appendix A)** and the **Picture Book Bibliography (B-5 in Appendix B)** and **Short Story Appeal Terms Bibliography (B-6 in Appendix B on the CD-ROM)** to help with the task of selecting materials appropriate for each activity.

Whole-Group-Appeal Terms:

a. Select two picture books (be sure these books are very different in feel from each other). Two possibilities are *Scaredy Squirrel* by Melanie Watt (Kids Can Press, 2008) and *Coming On Home Soon* by Jacqueline Woodson, Illustrated by E. B. Lewis (G. P. Putnam's Sons, 2004).

b. Read the first book aloud to your audience, then use an **Appeal Terms Worksheet (A-5 in Appendix A)** to assign appeal terms to the story elements. Finally, discuss its special features.

c. Read the second book aloud and do the same.

d. Discuss the differences between the two books and the specific ways in which each book creates a very different reading experience for the reader. (Be sure to touch briefly upon the illustrations and how they contribute to defining the appeal of each of the books' story elements.)

e. Now, break the whole group into pairs and give each pair of teachers five additional picture books and five more **Appeal Terms Worksheets (A-5 in Appendix A)**. Have them work in pairs to read the five books, assign appeal terms to the story elements, and discuss the special features of each book.

f. Re-gather the group and discuss.

Alternatively, if you have the time to do so, you might use short stories to do the same activity. For the read-alouds, use *Visit* by Walter Dean Myers and *Snowbound* by Lois Lowry. Both are from the anthology *Necessary Noise: Stories About Our Families as They Really Are*, edited by Michael Cart (Joanna Cotler Books, 2003). Then provide an assortment of short stories for each pair to read together.

Materials for the Whole-Group-Appeal Terms Activity:
- an assortment of picture books (see previously listed selection criteria)
- an assortment of short story anthologies (see previously listed selection criteria)

- **Appeal Terms Worksheets (A-5 in Appendix A)**

Appeal Terms Carousel

a. Label four tables: Pace, Tone, Characters or Characterization, Story Line.
b. Ahead of time (and using the **Picture Book Bibliography, B-5 in Appendix B** if you so desire), select four picture books that best illustrate four *different* appeal terms adjectives for each story element. For example, the table labeled Characters or Characterization will have four books on it, one with quirky characters, one with introspective characters, one with well-developed characters, and one with familiar characters.
c. Provide each table with four index cards, each one labeled with one of the four different appeal terms for that table's story element. (So the Characters/Characterization table from this example will have four index cards on it: quirky characters, introspective characters, well-developed characters, and familiar characters).
d. Rotate groups of four from table to table. Ask each person to read all four books. Then ask them to decide as a group which index card (appeal term) goes with which book.
e. Rotate each group through each table.
f. Guide a whole-group discussion.

Alternatively, if time allows, you might use short stories to do the same activity. If time is an issue, cut down the number of appeal terms per table from four to two, thereby requiring attendees to read fewer short stories. Ideally, and as yet an additional option, you might ask attendees to do some prereading and tailor the physical specifics to suit this particular scenario.

Materials for the Appeal Terms Carousel Activity
- one sign for each story element table
- sixteen index cards
- sixteen picture books or eight short stories (see previously listed selection criteria)

Closing Appeal Terms Activities

1. Sorting and/or Collapsing the Vocabulary of Appeal
2. Broadening the Vocabulary of Appeal
3. Selecting Appeal Terms to Teach

The activities in this section return to the vocabulary of appeal and demonstrate the vocabulary-building potential of teaching appeal terms concepts to students. Attendees are asked to play with the vocabulary by sorting and/or collapsing it and then expanding it. The last activity in the section should result in a whole-group consensus as to which appeal terms students will be explicitly taught for each of the story elements and at what grade level. This is also where you will want to have a conversation about which appeal terms may need to be modified (and how) for ease of comprehension. You are highly encouraged to go through this appeal terms selection/

modification process with your colleagues not only so that they have direct input, but also so that there is no confusion as to when particular appeal terms will be introduced to students. Clearly setting up these expectations from the outset will prevent teaching overlap and the dreaded student protestation "We already did this."

1. Sorting and/or Collapsing the Vocabulary of Appeal

a. Label four tables: Pace, Tone, Characters or Characterization, Story Line.

b. Split attendees into four groups (one per story element) and seat each group at a different table.

c. Using the **Appeal Terms Worksheet (A-5 in Appendix A)**, write each appeal term on an index card and sort onto the appropriate story-element table.

d. Direct each group to sort/arrange/categorize/collapse the appeal terms for their assigned story element in whatever way they feel is appropriate.

e. Ask each group to share with the larger group. Encourage each group to explain the rationale they used to sort their terms. Be prepared for the following to possibly emerge: The group responsible for Pace may sort the terms into slow and fast categories, sometimes along a continuum from slowest to fastest, and may, indeed, suggest additional terms to fill out the Pace continuum. The group responsible for Tone may sort the terms into light and dark, also sometimes on a continuum from lightest to darkest. The group responsible for Story Line may select the broader terms (i.e., action oriented, character centered, event/issue oriented, and setting oriented) and sort the other terms under each of these. The group responsible for Characters/Characterization may be tempted to collapse terms more than the other groups. For example, familiar, lifelike, realistic, and recognizable may be collapsed into one and well developed and well drawn may be considered much the same. Where the remaining terms for Characters/Characterization are sorted may become rather an issue for debate.

f. Distribute several **Appeal Terms Worksheets (A-5 in Appendix A)** to each table for use during the next part.

g. In this next and most important step, elicit cross-conversation and connection making between the story elements by guiding the discussion with the following questions while encouraging people to refer to specific appeal terms on the worksheet:

   i. What kind of tone(s) might you expect in a story with a breakneck pace? Why?

   ii. Why might you not expect a terrifically introspective character to surface in a high-octane mystery/thriller with an action-oriented story line?

   iii. What kind(s) of characters/characterization would you expect to find in a story with a character-centered story line? Why?

   iv. What kind of pace would you expect to find in a character-centered story line versus a story line that is action oriented? Why?

   v. In what types of story lines might you expect to find darker tones? Why?

   vi. Are there any particular kinds of characters you might expect to find in stories with darker tones? Why?

Note: You are not looking for steadfast right or wrong answers here, and broad generalizations are rarely useful; however, the conversation generated by these types of questions will guide people to apply their newly acquired understanding of the vocabulary of appeal across the story elements. Additionally, the questions will almost certainly generate healthy appeal terms debate among your colleagues. This debate should force deeper thought about appeal terms and their usefulness to the goal of advancing a more thorough understanding of how authors create specific reading experiences for their readers. This should serve to cement the concept of appeal terms for workshop attendees.

Materials for the Sorting and/or Collapsing the Vocabulary of Appeal Activity
- one sign for each story element table
- eighty-eight index cards, one for each of the appeal terms listed on the **Appeal Terms Worksheet (A-5 in Appendix A)**
- four or five **Appeal Terms Worksheets (A-5 in Appendix A)** for each table

2. Broadening the Vocabulary of Appeal

a. Label four tables: Pace, Tone, Characters or Characterization, Story Line.
b. Split attendees into four groups (one per story element) and seat each group at a different table.
c. Using the **Appeal Terms Worksheet (A-5 in Appendix A)**, select five appeal terms for each story element and write each of these at the top of a separate index card.
d. Direct each group to come up with as many synonyms for each of the appeal terms as they can. These should be written on the appropriate index cards.
e. Ask each group to share with the larger group and perhaps suggest to other groups additional synonyms that may have been overlooked.

Materials for the Broadening the Vocabulary of Appeal Activity
- one sign for each story element table
- five index cards for each table (with one preselected appeal term written on each)

3. Selecting Appeal Terms to Teach

Drawing on the last two activities, you and your colleagues should now have a conversation about which appeal terms to teach at each of the grade levels in your school. This should be a whole-group activity, with you being the official recorder of any consensus that is reached.

a. Provide each attendee with an **Appeal Terms Worksheet (A-5 in Appendix A)**.
b. Using either a projected Word document or chart paper, go through each of the appeal terms under each of the story elements on the worksheet.
c. For each, determine the following:
   i. whether it will be explicitly taught
   ii. the grade level in which it will be introduced and first taught
   iii. whether it will need to be modified for lower grades (this is where the work done with the synonyms for appeal terms will come in handy)

   d. Assure your colleagues that once you have had the time to collate responses, they will receive a complete document with all the information culled from this session available to them.

Book Hook Workshop Activities for the English Language Arts Department

Introducing the Workshop

An opening note: At the end of the day, the writing of Book Hooks is a kind of writing. Anyone who has taught writing will attest to the fact that it is an incredibly challenging endeavor. Merely competent writing requires the teaching of a lengthy and horrendously tedious list of language usage skills and rules. Good writing goes on to incorporate more complex questions of craft, but superior writing requires guidance in the development of a personal style and voice that is rarely, if ever, teachable by formula.

Much as with reading (and anything else we wish to master), the unvarnished truth of it is that the best way to improve writing is to practice it tirelessly. Fortunately, reading also helps greatly. Book Hooks are no exception. For this very reason, the two most important things you can do ahead of time to prepare for this workshop are: (1) Write Book Hooks for books you have read and (2) familiarize yourself with the Book Hooks (B-7 in Appendix B).

To be more specific: The more Book Hooks you write, the better. Aside from the obvious reasons for wanting to do this, it will help you to clarify for others the challenges they may encounter in writing them themselves and in subsequently teaching Book Hook writing to their students. As for the reading of Book Hooks, as you read each of the ones provided in this book, be sure to address the following questions: What works? Why? What doesn't work? Why not?

Finally, it is probably safe to assume from the outset of your workshop on Book Hook writing that the English Language Arts teachers who will be in attendance already employ a number of techniques to teach writing to their students. In fact, a part of what you are going to want to do in this workshop is collaborate with your colleagues to find the best ways to incorporate some of these very techniques into the teaching of Book Hook writing.

The activities for the Book Hook Writing Workshop are divided into three categories: Introductory, Middle, and Closing. A number of activities are suggested for each section of the workshop. Ideally, you would have several sessions to cover all the necessary ground. Where possible, materials are provided. In the instances in which the material required for an activity is copyrighted, it has not been included here. All the necessary information is provided for you to locate said material on your own. In most cases, the use of copyrighted material as part of a workshop in an educational environment is considered fair use provided a full citation is included. Where the use of picture books (or parts of longer books) is called for, you are encouraged to either do read-alouds, purchase inexpensive paperback copies, or borrow multiple copies from your local public library. Some of the suggested activities may require you to preread materials in order that you may better understand what you are conveying to your audience. Where this is the case, it is so noted.

Introductory Book Hook Activities

1. The Book Hook Form
2. The Book Hook Worksheet Form
3. So, What is a Book Hook and How Do I Write One?
4. Book Hooks vs. Plot-Based Descriptions
5. Book Hooks vs. Blurbs
6. Book Hooks vs. Reviews

Middle Book Hook Activities

1. Favorite Picture Books
2. *Winston the Book Wolf* Book Hooks
3. Writing Book Hooks for Favorite Picture Books
4. Writing Book Hooks for Short Stories

Closing Book Hook Activities

1. A Rubric for Book Hooks
2. Customizing the Book Hook
3. Formalizing an Official Book Hook Procedure
4. Book Hook Bulletin Boards

Introductory Book Hook Activities

1. The Book Hook Form
2. The Book Hook Worksheet Form
3. So, What Is a Book Hook and How Do I Write One?
4. Plot-Based Descriptions vs. Book Hooks
5. Book Hooks vs. Blurbs and Reviews

This is the part of the workshop during which attendees are better familiarized with Book Hooks. As such, the activities are primarily centered on defining or describing Book Hooks. Beyond this, it will be helpful for your colleagues to compare and contrast Book Hooks to plot-based descriptions, book blurbs, and book reviews. Throughout, keep emphasizing the ultimate goal of Book Hook writing: the systematic sharing of reading throughout your school. Remember: You are selling the idea of Book Hook writing and sharing. Depending on how much time you have for the workshop, try one (or several) of the introductory activities that follow.

1. **The Book Hook Form.** Distribute the **Book Hook** form **(A-1 in Appendix A)** and generate a conversation about incorporating the writing of Book Hooks into independent reading class time so that students can systematically share what they have read with each other. This is where you will want to share with colleagues the Book Hooks you have written and keep in the library for your students to browse when they are in search of their next book. Explain that the more students talk to each other about the books they have read, the more they read. Include any anecdotes you may have that illustrate this point (i.e., students coming in with friends to swap books).

2. **The Book Hook Worksheet Form.** Initiate a conversation about the need your colleagues may encounter to modify or scaffold the writing of Book Hooks. Then distribute the **Book Hook Worksheet (A-6 in Appendix A)**. Use the collaborative opportunity offered by the workshop setting to modify the worksheet as your colleagues see fit. The more input you get from others, the more likely they are to adopt your proposal.

3. **So, What Is a Book Hook and How Do I Write One?** Spend a few minutes defining Book Hooks. Distribute **Appeal Terms Worksheet (A-5 in Appendix A)** and **So, What Is a Book Hook and How Do I Write One? (A-7 in Appendix A)** and discuss.

4. **Plot-Based Descriptions vs. Book Hooks.** Distribute **Plot-Based Descriptions vs. Book Hooks (A-8 in Appendix A)**. Discuss the following:
   a. What do the Book Hooks provide for readers that the summaries don't?
   b. Look at each of the Book Hooks. What particular words caught your eye in each?
   c. How is the plot of each book conveyed in the Book Hooks?

5. **Book Hooks vs. Blurbs and Reviews.** For this part of the workshop, you will want attendees to read, compare, and contrast a number of Book Hooks with their corresponding blurbs and book reviews. If you have written Book Hooks of your own, feel free to use these and track down the necessary book reviews and book blurbs. If you prefer, use Book Hooks and materials suggested as follows.
   a. *Unwind* by Neal Shusterman
      ○ Book Hook (see **Book Hooks, B-7 in Appendix B**)
      ○ Ned Vizzini's *New York Times* book review of *Unwind*, available at http://www.nytimes.com/2008/03/16/books/review/Vizzini-t.html
      ○ Library Media Connection (January, 2008) review of *Unwind*
      ○ *Unwind* book blurb, available on SyFy book blog at http://www.syfy.co .uk/blog/books/unwind-by-neil-shusterman
   b. *The Seer of Shadows* by Avi
      ○ Book Hook (see **Book Hooks, B-7 in Appendix B**)
      ○ Horn Book (May/June, 2008) book review of *The Seer of Shadows*
      ○ *The Seer of Shadows* book blurb available on the Harper Collins website at http://www.harpercollins.com/browseinside/index.aspx?isbn13=9780060 000158
   c. *The* Eye of the Crow *by Shane Peacock*
      ○ Book Hook (see **Book Hooks, B-7 in Appendix B**)
      ○ Horn Book (Spring, 2008) book review of *The Eye of the Crow* OR
      ○ Jeffrey Canton's July 2007 review for the Quill & Quire website at http:// www.quillandquire.com/books_young/review.cfm?review_id=5640
      ○ *The Eye of the Crow* book blurb available via Flickr at http://www.flickr .com/photos/theverynk/2535011290/#/photos/theverynk/2535011290/ lightbox/

Following a perusal of the materials, the discussion should focus on answering the following questions:

- What do the Book Hooks provide for readers that neither reviews nor the blurbs provide?
- Which reviews employ appeal terms? What effect does this have on the impact of the review?
- How is plot conveyed in the reviews? In the book blurbs?
- Which blurbs are most effective? Why?
- Which reviews are most effective? Why?
- What are the similarities between book blurbs and Book Hooks? What are the differences?
- What are the similarities between book reviews and Book Hooks? What are the differences?

Middle Book Hook Activities

1. Favorite Picture Books
2. *Winston the Book Wolf* Book Hooks
3. Writing Book Hooks for Favorite Picture Books
4. Writing Book Hooks for Short Stories

This is the part of the workshop during which your colleagues begin to try their hand at writing Book Hooks themselves. As with any writing activity, the going is often slow in the beginning stages. To help this process along, you may want to give attendees the option of working in small groups (unless they prefer to work alone). In order for the first suggested activity in this section to be most effective, you will want to reach out to colleagues in advance of the day of the workshop. Ask each attendee to bring a favorite picture book to the workshop. (This book can be either a personal favorite or one they enjoyed reading to a child.) These books will be used for a Do Now of sorts and will serve as lead-ins to the next set of activities. Middle Book Hook activities 2 through 4 will require you to provide a selection of picture books and short stories. Consider using the picture books provided by your colleagues, as this will increase their ownership of the workshop and encourage participation. You can also refer to the **Picture Book Bibliography** and **Short Story Bibliography (B-5 and B-6** in **Appendix B and on the CD-ROM respectively)** for guidance. Where specific materials are required, necessary information has been provided. While picture books are fast reads, short stories may take a little more time. As such, if at all possible, you may want to ask your workshop attendees to preread some of the required materials. In addition to the materials specified below, each attendee will need a copy of the **Appeal Terms Worksheet (A-5 in Appendix A).**

1. **Favorite Picture Books.** Start the workshop by asking for one or two volunteers to read aloud their favorite picture book. Ask the volunteer(s) to explain what hooked them on the book. Guide the conversation in the direction of identifying the appeal of each of the story elements. As before, touch briefly on the role of the illustrations in augmenting appeal elements. Next, pair people up and ask them to read each other's favorite picture books and discuss their hooks and appeal. Set favorites aside and lead into the next activity.

2. *Winston the Book Wolf* **Book Hooks**. For this activity, you will need the following:
   - a copy of *Winston the Book Wolf* written by Marni McGee and illustrated by Ian Beck (London: Bloomsbury Children's Books, 2006)
   - copies of the **Appeal Terms Worksheet (A-5 in Appendix A)** to distribute at the beginning of the workshop
   - copies of **Book Hooks for *Winston the Book Wolf* (B-8 in Appendix B)** to distribute after the read-aloud
     The following steps are provided as a guide:
   a. Distribute copies of the **Appeal Terms Worksheet (A-5 in Appendix A)**.
   b. As you read *Winston the Book Wolf* aloud to your colleagues, ask them to think about which appeal terms they would use to describe its various story elements. Have them jot these down.
   c. Once you are done reading the story, elicit the assigned appeal terms and discuss.
   d. Either in small groups or singly, have the attendees write Book Hooks for the book.
   e. Share Book Hooks and discuss the following questions:
      - Which of the Book Hooks work best? Why?
      - Which ones need tweaking? Why? What specific adjustments do they need?
      - Which Book Hook paints the best picture of the book? Why?
   f. Distribute copies of **Book Hooks for *Winston the Book Wolf* (B-8 in Appendix B)** and address the questions above.
3. **Writing Book Hooks for Favorite Picture Books**. Return to your colleagues' favorite picture books by asking them to write Book Hooks for them. Share.
4. **Writing Book Hooks for Short Stories**. In advance of this particular activity, you will want to ask your colleagues to bring a selection of short stories for discussion. As you will be conducting this workshop with English Language Arts teachers, they should be encouraged to bring the stories they read with their students. In this way, there will already be a commonality of reading experiences from which to begin working. Additionally, the familiarity that comes with reading something more than once (as most teachers do over the years with their students) will make it easier to shift the focus from literary analysis to appeal terms and Book Hook writing for the short stories. Besides, the advantage of having teachers assign appeal terms and write Book Hooks for stories they teach will make it easier for them to teach both these skills to their students using the very materials all their students will have read in class. Finally, working with familiar material will serve as a good launch pad for introducing two new stories to the group later in the workshop.
   The following steps are provided as a guide:
   a. Divide attendees into pairs using the short stories they bring to the workshop. This will probably turn out to be pairs of same-grade ELA teachers, as most English departments have set material they cover with each grade.

b. Ask the pairs to select one story from those they brought with them.

c. Ask the pairs to discuss/assign appeal terms for each of the story elements of each of the short stories. They should also come up with one or two synonyms for each of the appeal terms.

d. Have attendees distill the plots of their stories down to one or two sentences maximum.

e. Before having people actually write a Book Hook for their story, remind them of the following:
   ○ In order to write a good Book Hook, they will have to figure out and verbalize precisely what hooked them into the story.
   ○ The best-written Book Hooks concisely convey the feel of a story.
   ○ Book Hooks carefully weave appeal terms (and their synonyms) throughout the distilled plot summary.
   ○ Book Hooks should not be longer than two paragraphs.
   ○ Book Hooks close by identifying the three appeal terms that give the best snapshot of the story.

f. Share with your colleagues the Hooks for *Visit* by Walter Dean Myers and *Snowbound* by Lois Lowry (both are available in the **Short Story Bibliography, B-6 in Appendix B on CD-ROM**). Point out the following:
   ○ their brevity
   ○ the focus on the feel of the stories
   ○ the limited amount of plot summary

g. Have colleagues write Hooks for their chosen short stories. Then share Book Hooks and discuss.

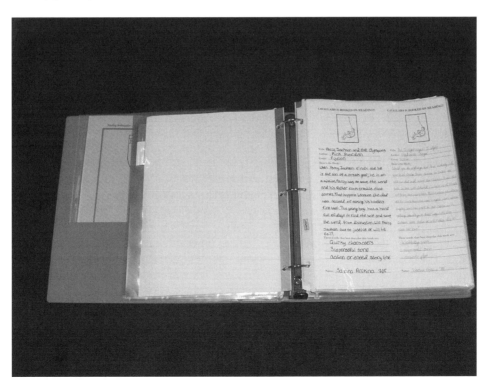

The Book Hook Binder

Closing Book Hook Activities

1. A Rubric for Book Hooks
2. Customizing the Book Hook
3. Formalizing an Official Book Hook Procedure
4. Book Hook Bulletin Boards

Dear English Language Arts Teacher,

In an attempt to improve the reading culture in our building, we spent the summer looking at ways to increase our students' pleasure reading. We also devoted time to devising a new system to monitor this reading.

The driving philosophy behind the new system is to encourage students to read for pleasure and to share their reading interests with others. The Book Hook Binder becomes a living document to which students continuously add entries and read recommendations by their peers.

Book Hook Binder Procedures:
1. Each ELA teacher receives one binder for all of his or her ELA classes.
2. Within this binder, there are dividers for every student, as well as sheet protectors for the Book Hook sheets.
3. Each student will have a section within the Book Hook Binder for his or her entries.
4. Any time students completes a book (any book of their choosing that they enjoyed), they complete a Book Hook (each sheet holds two Book Hooks). You determine if you want to collect these prior to their inclusion within the Book Hook binder or if you would rather have students place them directly in the binder themselves. In either case, please be aware that as this is the new way in which we are monitoring students' independent reading, this is something that should be closely supervised by you.
5. A digital version of the Book Hook will be e-mailed to you. Feel free to utilize this format, as it facilitates importing pictures of book covers, incorporates technology, and may motivate more reluctant readers. If you choose to use the digital forms, provisions will have to be made for printing them.
6. The front of each binder contains several sample sheets already filled out and enough blank ones for you to get started.
7. When the students complete their summer reading Book Hooks for the first bulletin board of the school year, consider having them transfer the information onto a Book Hook sheet and filing it in the classroom binder. This will become their first entry for the coming school year.
8. Consider creating a section in the Book Hook binder for your own independent reading entries. All the research shows that modeling your own strong reading habits will motivate your students to read more.

School-wide Extensions of the Book Hook Binders
1. It is our hope that our students will be involved in making future recommendations for our Spring Into Reading list, as well as summer reading. At various points throughout the year, the Literacy Committee will be asking you to forward especially well-written Book Hooks for inclusion in future book lists.
2. In addition, we would like to move in the direction of having a school-wide Book Hook binder in the library. Please consider photocopying those entries that are especially well written and forwarding them to the librarian so that she can add them to a growing collection of her own Book Hooks.

In closing, please remember that this is a work in progress, and we very much welcome any feedback or suggestions you may have to improve this for the future.

This will only succeed with your support and enthusiasm.

Sincerely,

Figure 4.   Book Hook Binder Letter

School Name
Principal

ADMINISTRATIVE CIRCULAR #9

Book Hook Binder Procedure
1. Each E.L.A. teacher receives one binder for all of their E.L.A. classes.
2. Within this binder, there are dividers for every student, as well as sheet protectors for the Book Hook sheets.
3. Each student will have a section within the Book Hook Binder for their entries.
4. Any time a student completes a book (any book of their choosing that they enjoyed reading), they complete a Book Hook (each sheet holds two entries). You determine if you want to collect these prior to their inclusion within the Book Hook Binder or, if you would rather have students place them directly in the Book Hook Binder themselves. In either case, please be aware, that as this is the new way in which we are monitoring students' independent reading, this is something that should be closely supervised by you.
5. A digital version of the Book Hook sheets will be e-mailed to your DOE e-mail account. Feel free to utilize this format as it facilitates importing pictures of book covers, incorporates technology and may motivate more reluctant readers. If you choose to use the digital forms, provisions will have to be made for printing them.
6. The front of each binder contains several sample Book Hooks already filled out and enough blank ones for you to get started.
7. Consider creating a section in the Book Hook Binder for your own independent reading entries. All the research shows that modeling your own reading habits will motivate your students to read more.

Figure 5.   Sample Procedure Proposal

Student Book Hooks Bulletin Board

In this part of the Book Hook workshop, you will be working closely with your colleagues to iron out the details of what tools will be used to teach Book Hook writing in your school. As such, the activities in this section will require you to elicit (and keep track of) suggestions for customizing the Book Hook to suit your teachers' needs and coming up with a schoolwide procedure for implementing Book Hooks in your school.

1. **A Rubric for Book Hooks**. Distribute and review the **Book Hook Rubric (A-9 in Appendix A)**. Decide (with your colleagues' input) if you like this particular rubric. Elicit and keep track of suggestions for modifications. Make the Book Hook Rubric your own by tailoring it to your school's and teachers' needs.

2. **Customizing the Book Hook**. Distribute and review **The Book Hook (A-1 in Appendix A)**. Elicit and keep track of suggestions for modifications. Some questions you might want to discuss:
   ◦ Do you want the school name on the Book Hook?
   ◦ Do you want an image on the Book Hook? What will it be?
   ◦ Would you prefer to have one Book Hook per page or do you like the idea of having two to a page?

3. **Formalizing an Official Book Hook Procedure.** Most schools have policy and procedure manuals. Using the **Book Hook Binder Letter (Figure 4)** and **Sample Procedure Proposal (Figure 5)** as guides, craft a rough draft of a Book Hook writing and sharing procedure for your school. Administration can take or leave the suggested procedure but may be more inclined to do the former if it is already sketched out for them. Be sure to elicit input from your colleagues about what to include in the formalized procedure. The more people contribute to the creation of policies and procedures, the more of a stake they have in actually following them.

4. **Book Hooks Bulletin Boards.** One of the best ways to achieve success with the Book Hook writing endeavor is to provide teachers with the materials needed to create a bulletin board of Book Hooks written by their students. Offer your colleagues blank Book Hooks run off on neon-colored paper so that as their students write Book Hooks, the best of them can be transferred to the bright paper and used to create classroom and hallway bulletin boards.

Part Two

On to the Students

Your proposal to administration has been accepted, you have delivered the appeal terms and Book Hook writing workshops to your colleagues, and you have provided all the materials they will need to implement a Book Hook binder in their classrooms. At this point, there will be those teachers that go back to their classrooms and fly with all of this on their own, and others who will seek additional collaboration with you. While most ELA teachers will probably want to personalize how they teach appeal terms and Book Hooks to their students, your willingness to collaborate further will insure that your level of commitment to the endeavor is clear. Then there is the notion that providing several classroom activities for colleagues to tweak as they see fit will almost assuredly be viewed as helpful. As such, this section offers a number of ideas for teaching appeal terms and Book Hook writing to students. Use these as suggestions (rather than as scripted edicts) and encourage anyone with whom you share them to collaborate with you on further tailoring and developing them to suit their specific needs. As with any other initiative you suggest, make yourself available to coteach (if your colleague should want you to). Keep well at the forefront the ultimate goal of all this: establishing a system for students (and teachers) to consistently share their reading.

Colleagues embracing this initiative should begin by setting up their Book Hook binder with one section for each of their students and determining a classroom procedure for incorporating it into their reading and writing routines. They should discuss the new procedure with their students and show them the Book Hook binder before beginning any of the lessons.

Note: Some of the activities in this section are identical to some of those suggested for the workshops. Where this is the case, it is noted and you will be referred to the appropriate page(s) in Part I.

Activities to Teach Appeal Terms to Students

1. The Reading Survey Lesson
2. Introducing the Experience of Appeal Terms (Lesson)
3. Appeal Terms Defined/Assigning Appeal Terms (ongoing)
4. Expanding the Vocabulary of Appeal (ongoing)
5. Appeal Terms Carousel (see: Part I, pages 1 to 30)
6. Using the Arts to Deepen the Understanding of Appeal Terms

With the exception of starting with the Reading Survey and the second lesson (Introducing the Experience of Appeal Terms), the activity/lesson ideas listed here (and detailed in the following pages) need not be addressed in any particular order. In general, the process of teaching students appeal terms is largely one of exposing them to a new vocabulary to discuss their reading experiences. Fortunately, many of the actual appeal terms are words with which your students will already be familiar (i.e., *fast, creepy, realistic*). The newness here will be in learning how these familiar words can be used to describe the story elements of pace, tone, characterization, and story line. In order for this endeavor to be successful, they will have to first learn the vocabulary of appeal. In order to fully internalize this vocabulary, students will need to be given regular opportunities to practice assigning appeal terms to the story elements of what they are reading. With practice will come proficiency. This practice, however, need not be unduly onerous. Keep well in mind the curricular expectations that govern the lives of your colleagues and hasten to assure them that the appeal terms reinforcement their students will need can easily be incorporated into whatever works of literature they are already teaching. Once the broad concepts of appeal are taught, the application of the terms can be as brief or as lengthy a periodic activity as your colleagues see fit. Word walls and posters of the story elements and their corresponding appeal terms can serve as constant visual reinforcement, and even referring to these in passing can serve to further gel appeal terms concepts for students. Of course, where the library is concerned, posters of the appeal terms (**B-9, What Appeals to You? In Appendix B**) should be on prominent display and referred to regularly when students come in looking for books to read. The more consistently your students encounter the terms, the more likely it is that they will internalize the concept of appeal and begin to use it naturally and without prompting. Finally, continue to emphasize the idea that both appeal terms and Book Hook writing are being implemented to increase the systematic opportunities students will be given to share what they have read with each other.

1. **The Reading Survey Lesson**. Using the **Reading Survey (A-3 in Appendix A)** to introduce the concept of appeal terms to your students offers a number of advantages. To start, it requires them to think about their reading preferences in a new way and exposes them to the story elements they will be asked to keep in mind any time they evaluate a book for its appeal. More importantly, however, it establishes the ownership we want them to take of their reading. We are not telling them what they like to read. We want them to tell us what they like to read, and in order for them to be able to do so intelligently (and so that we and their peers may successfully make recommendations), they are being asked to be specific in how they describe what they like to read. To be plainly clear: Any student truly interested in finding a good book to read will have to be motivated and taught by her teachers to be equally interested in doing the legwork involved in clearly describing what she is looking for. Our responsibility is to assist our students in learning how to do this, not to do it for them.

   As long as you are on the subject of discussing books intelligently, take the opportunity to make a case against students using the word *interesting* to describe a book they read and liked. Explain that *interesting* is only helpful if one goes on to say precisely *what* was interesting about the book he or she just read. Finally, before the students actually get down to the task of filling out the survey, be sure to clarify that this survey is meant to glean their general preferences. As we all know, avid readers may enjoy a variety of books with varying appeal (depending on what they are in the mood for). Most of us, however, have preferences to which we gravitate, and even the most reluctant readers will at least have very definite reading dislikes. You may be pleasantly surprised to find that your students are excited that they are being asked to be honest about not only what they like but also what they dislike. Share with them that often it is easier to know what to recommend by knowing clearly what is disliked than knowing only vaguely what is liked. Use the steps that follow as a guide for the Reading Survey Lesson.

(Note: Ideally, this is a two-period activity done at the beginning of the school year.)

Explain that completed surveys will be filed at the beginning of each student's section in the class Book Hook binder. Be prepared to put a positive spin on the protestations of any reluctant readers. This activity was designed with them very much in mind. We can move them away from their stance of reluctance by expressing a genuine interest in helping them figure out what their reading likes and dislikes are. Besides, the idea that students are doing this more for their peers than for the adults in the building can serve as a powerful motivator for them. (See Figure 6 on page 34 for lesson plan.)

2. **Introducing the Experience of Appeal Terms Lesson.** The primary goal here is to model for your students how appeal terms work to describe the story elements of books. Materials necessary for this activity: **Appeal Terms Worksheet (A-5 in Appendix A)** and an assortment of picture books of your choosing. Refer to the **Appeal Terms Glossary (B-10 in Appendix B)** for definitions of the story elements. (See Figure 7 on page 35 for lesson plan.)

3. **Appeal Terms Defined/Assigning Appeal Terms (ongoing).** Defining all the appeal terms as they apply to the story elements is something that will take place over time, ideally, as the students need clarification of particular terms. As stated earlier, most of the actual words will already be familiar to students. In the event that additional definition is needed, use the **Glossary of Appeal Terms (B-10 in Appendix B)**. It is suggested that teachers spend some time overtly defining and illustrating the more complex vocabulary of appeal using picture books, short stories, or even brief passages that are good examples (see the **Picture Book** and **Short Story Bibliographies, B-5 and B-6 in Appendix B,** as well as the **Index** to determine what picture books to use to teach each of the appeal terms). Alternatively, teachers can modify the list of appeal terms to include only those they feel their students need to learn at first. For additional reading material, teachers should use literature that is read as part of the ELA curriculum, since it will lend itself to being discussed using appeal terms. For ongoing assigning of the terms, teachers may also choose to use the abbreviated list of appeal terms provided on the **Appeal Bookmarks (A-10 in Appendix A)**. Run these off on brightly

Grade Level: 6–12   **Lesson Duration:** 2 class periods

Essential Question: What is the common vocabulary we can use to describe our reading preferences?

Learning Outcomes: The students will be able to identify particular personal reading preferences.

AASL Standards for the 21st Century Learner:
4.4.1—Identify own areas of interest

	Procedure	Resources
Mini Lesson	Introduce the Reading Survey and explain its purposes: • you want to know what your students like to read • you would like them to describe what they like to read using specific terms • it will serve as a strong starting place for them to share their reading preferences with each other and find classmates with similar reading tastes.	(A-3) Reading Survey Interactive whiteboard to display survey
Guided Practice	Model taking the survey for your students, explaining as you go along.	
Independent Practice	Distribute one Reading Survey to each student and have them fill it out.	
Sharing/ Reflection	Have students find peers with similar reading likes and dislikes and record their names on their own surveys.	
Assessment:	Students answer the following questions for homework: • What did you learn about your own reading preferences from completing this survey? • What did you learn about the reading preferences about some of your friends? • What is the advantage of knowing which of your classmates have similar reading preference?	

Follow Up/Extension: Students file their Reading Surveys in their own sections of the classroom Book Hook Binder.

Figure 6.   The Reading Survey Lesson

    colored cardstock, cut each sheet into three bookmarks, and get students in the habit of taking one and using it any time they begin to read a new book.

4. **Expanding the Vocabulary of Appeal (ongoing).** In preparation for having your students learn how to write Book Hooks, you will want to guide them in broadening the vocabulary of appeal so that they have a wider array of terms to choose from when they get down to the task of writing Book Hooks for the books they have read. This is nothing more than building a list of synonyms and brief phrases for each of the appeal terms and keeping track of them so that they are readily available when the students need them. In addition to building vocabulary, this ongoing activity will help them eliminate tired and overused words from their Book Hooks. Encourage the students to be creative and stretch as they search for colorful and enticing vocabulary to describe their reading experiences. Building on an existing Appeal Terms

Grade Level: 6–12   **Lesson Duration:** 2 class periods

Essential Question: How do appeal terms help us to accurately describe the experience of reading a book?

Learning Outcomes: The students will be able to use appeal terms to describe the pace, tone, story line, and characters/characterization for two picture books.

AASL Standards for the 21st Century Learner:
4.1.1—Read, view, and listen for pleasure and personal growth.
4.1.2—Read widely and fluently to make connections with self, the world, and previous reading.

	Procedure	Resources
Mini Lesson	Define each of the story elements: • Pace • Tone • Story line • Characters/characterization	Refer to: B-10, Appeal Terms Glossary
Guided Practice	• Read aloud: *Olivia* by Ian Falconer • Have students set up a T-chart on loose-leaf paper labeled *Olivia* and *Cherry and Olive*. • Elicit from the students what adjectives they would use to describe the book *Olivia*. Record responses on a T-chart under the heading *Olivia*. • Distribute the Appeal Terms Worksheet and explain: "These terms will help us clearly and uniformly describe the experience of reading *Olivia*." • Elicit and assign appeal terms to the four story elements. Discuss as you go. Have students record these in the *Olivia* side of their T-charts.	*Olivia* by Ian Falconer T-chart on whiteboard for whole-group work A-5, Appeal Terms Worksheet
Independent Practice	• Read aloud: *Cherry and Olive* by Benjamin Lacombe. • In pairs, have the students complete the *Cherry and Olive* side of their T-charts. • In pairs, students assign appeal terms for *Cherry and Olive* using the Appeal Terms Worksheet.	*Cherry and Olive* by Benjamin Lacombe
Sharing/ Reflection	Whole-group discussion: • What appeal terms did you assign to the four story elements of *Cherry and Olive*? Why? • What makes these two books different from each other? • Which book did you like better? Why?	
Assessment: Students read trough a number of preselected picture books and explain which ones they think "feel" like *Olivia* and which ones they think "feel" like *Cherry and Olive*.		

Follow-Up/Extension: Students continue to read picture books and assign appeal terms to the four story elements.

Figure 7.   Introducing the Experience of Appeal Terms Lesson

word wall is a perfect and simple enough way to keep track of this new vocabulary.

5. **Appeal Terms Carousel (see: Part I, pages 1 to 30).** This activity will help your students deepen their understanding of the concept of appeal by requiring them to categorize books they read by various different appeal terms.

6. **Using the Arts to Deepen the Understanding of Appeal Terms.** One of the ways in which students can be helped to internalize the various appeal terms is to use both the visual and performing arts to drive home specific appeal concepts. It is hardly a stretch to say that where writers use words, artists use color and light in painting and photography to create specific experiences for their audiences. Nor is it far fetched to claim that music does very much the same for listeners with pace and tone. In fact, where music is concerned, tone and pace are critical to creating the feel of any given piece of music, and some song lyrics can have a number of the same appeal characteristics as short stories. Music paired with moving images creates powerful responses (think horror movie soundtracks), and surely the Disney classic *Fantasia* amply illustrated that music can most certainly elicit pictorial narrative. Where the arts and appeal terms are concerned, having fun with the endeavor is well in order. The best-case scenario is one in which students assign appeal terms to a variety of paintings, photographs, and music. Obviously, not all appeal terms will apply, and in the interest of clarity, the issue should not be forced.

While the connections between appeal terms and the arts are there for the making and pointing out, the wealth of material available for use here is positively overwhelming. Rather than making suggestions for specific material to use, the choice is left intentionally up to the teacher. Materials for which individual teachers have particular affinities will go much further in teaching the concepts than materials chosen with someone else's passions governing the choices. Wherever possible, cross-curricular collaborations with art and music teachers are strongly encouraged.

Finally, illustrations in the very best picture books contribute greatly to the enhancement of appeal and offer a perfect starting point for a discussion of the ways in which the visual arts pair with the verbal arts to create very definite reading experiences. Please note: This particular lesson presupposes familiarity with appeal terms for tone and some familiarity with styles of illustration. As such, it is recommended that an art teacher teach this particular lesson to a class with which (s)he has covered some of the material ahead of time as part of the art curriculum. (See Figure 8 on page 37 for lesson plan.)

Activities to Teach Book Hook Writing to Students

1. What's the Hook? (lesson)
2. *Visit* by Walter Dean Myers—What's the Hook? (lesson)
3. The Text Engagement Conversation and Reading Log Entries (ongoing)
4. Summarizing (lesson and ongoing)
5. Building a Book Hook (lesson and ongoing)

Grade Level: 6–12   **Lesson Duration:** 2 class periods

Essential Question: In what ways do picture book illustrations enhance the particular appeal of a story?

Learning Outcomes: Students will know and be able to identify characteristics of illustrations that make them best suited for the stories they illustrate.

AASL Standards for the 21st Century Learner:
4.1.3—Respond to literature and creative expressions of ideas in various formats and genres.

	Procedure	Resources
Mini Lesson	• Without reading the story, show the students several of the illustrations in *Scaredy Squirrel* by Melanie Watt. • Elicit adjectives that describe the illustrations. • Ask: "Just by looking at the illustrations, what kind of tone do you suspect this story might have? Why?" Discuss.	*Scaredy Squirrel* by Melanie Watt
Guided Practice	• Before reading, explain that you want the students to make pictures in their heads as you read. Explain that you will be asking them to describe these pictures in detail. • Without revealing the illustrations, read aloud *Coming on Home Soon* by Jacqueline Woodson. • Work with the students to assign appeal terms to the pace and tone of the story. (Pace: unhurried; tone: quiet.) • Ask: "Would you expect this story to have illustrations similar to those in *Scaredy Squirrel*? Why or why not?" Discuss. • Elicit what features they might expect this story's illustrations to have.	*Coming on Home Soon* by Jacqueline Woodson
Independent Practice	• Distribute one picture book to each pair of students. • In pairs, students read their picture books, paying close attention to the illustrations. • Students assign their books appeal terms for tone. • Students evaluate their picture book illustrations, saying if they go with the story and why or why not.	An assortment of picture books with varied illustrations. (enough to give one book to each pair of students).
Sharing/ Reflection	• Share Independent Practice Activity. • Ask: "What did you discover about picture book stories and their illustrations?" • Elicit explanations.	
Assessment: Collect work from Independent Practice and review.		

Follow-Up/Extension: Students read additional picture books and evaluate their illustrations for suitability, making suggestions for improvement if they feel the illustrations do not fit.

Figure 8.   The Appeal of Illustrations Lesson

The three main ingredients necessary for well-written Book Hooks are engagement with the text, familiarity with appeal terms, and writing skill. The last ingredient will only come with time and practice. Textual engagement is critical because without it, the writer of the Book Hook will not be able to successfully identify and convey the hook of any given story. In the best of all possible worlds, our students would be able to identify and skillfully convey the hooks of even those stories they did not enjoy reading, and this is surely a long-term goal worth having. Keep in mind, however, that the level of sophistication and maturity necessary to be able to detach from personal preferences sufficiently to be able to convey the potential appeal of something we dislike is not something we should expect adolescents to possess. This ability will have to be coaxed out of them and nurtured over time. Starting with forcing students to write Book Hooks for books and stories they did not enjoy reading is both pointless and counterproductive. The ultimate goal of Book Hook writing and sharing is to increase reading. Reading is not increased by attaching a writing assignment to an unpleasant reading experience. If anything, in fact, our insistence on having students write at length about everything they read (as a way of confirming that they have read it) has singlehandedly done more to discourage reading than all of our other academic misdeeds combined.

With all of that said, it will be necessary to read a variety of material with your students to get them started on Book Hook writing. Suffice it to say, a good dose of honesty and the use of short stories and picture books will go a very long way here. Start by reiterating the overall goal: Everyone reads more because they have learned how to define and find what they like to read. Explain that part of that defining process will continue to be one of elimination. By reading a variety of short stories and picture books, students will more quickly be able to both eliminate what does not appeal to them and figure out what does. In any event, they will learn how to engage with text using the vocabulary of appeal as a guide. This is why, before starting on Book Hook writing, students should have a strong foundation in using appeal terms and their synonyms. Finally, be honest. You will not be asking them to write extensively about full-length novels they disliked. Nor will you be asking them to wax rhapsodic over short stories and picture books they did not enjoy. You merely want them to be able to clearly identify the appeal of a given story in the service of eventually writing about books they love. It may help to clarify further in this way: Even if you are not at all personally partial to beige as a color, surely you can identify it when you see it.

One of the critical appeal concepts for students to understand when it comes to Book Hooks is that the same book (or story) can have a number of different hooks built into it and that individual readers may be hooked by any and/or all of these. The best way to convey this concept is to read a number of stories with your students with the express purpose of teaching them how to identify all of the stories' hooks. This process is much facilitated by bringing students back to the four story elements: pace, tone, story line, and characters/characterization. Aside from the actual craft of writing, each of these elements of a story gives an author an opportunity to hook readers. In turn, readers may be hooked by any and/or all of these elements as developed in a particular story. For this reason, the starting place for all Book Hook writing is in identifying the appeal of each of the story elements and, most importantly, figuring out which of the story elements are best developed—these, after all, will be what hook readers in the end.

Having accomplished the appeal identification task, Book Hook writing will next require your students to pinpoint and describe precisely how the author goes about using words (and words and illustrations in the case of picture books) to create a story that, for example, is shot through with a foreboding tone. This is where the teaching of Book Hook writing can easily turn into a study of the craft of writing and where studying writing in this way is a natural lead-in to learning how to be a better writer.

A note on reading materials to teach Book Hook Writing: **The Short Story Bibliography (B-6 in Appendix B on the CD-ROM)** and **The Picture Book Bibliography (B-5 in Appendix B)** are included as resources. In addition to these, specific short stories and picture books are recommended for use in the Book Hook writing activities and lessons that follow. Obviously, personal preference will trump any suggestions made here. What you will ultimately be modeling is the art of being able to identify the hooks and appeal of any given story—regardless of whether the story speaks to you. Book Hook writing is not about judging books. Book Hooks are about zeroing in on the key features of the story that constitute its appeal and then weaving them into a microsummary of the story in such a way as to enable the Book Hook reader who knows her reading preferences to decide if it is something she wants to read herself. If there are short stories and picture books you are passionate about, use them in place of the ones suggested, as they will make it easier for you to model Book Hook writing for your students.

Note: The first lesson below (See Figure 9 on page 40 for lesson plan.) is a general one to use with a variety of picture books as students learn to identify the particular hooks of different stories. Once they have become good at identifying the hooks, they can be moved on to doing the same with short stories. A number of the other lessons in this section focus on one particular short story: Walter Dean Myers's *Visit*. The advantage of using the same story to teach more than one lesson is that it establishes a clear progression of steps for students. In order to ultimately be able to write good Book Hooks, they will have to go through each of the steps taught in each of the lessons. As such, it makes sense to use one story to teach all of the steps. Clearly, *Visit* by Walter Dean Myers is not the only short story one might use to teach these lessons. (In fact, for the lower grades, you will want to use something else—and picture books are always a good idea.) *Visit* was selected because it is powerfully written and it perfectly illustrates a number of points we want our students to internalize about Book Hook writing. In the end, the short story and picture book selections for these lessons are a matter of personal choice.

1. **What's the Hook?** The best way to help students learn how to determine the hook of a story is to read and discuss which of a story's elements are best developed and used by the author to grab readers. Doing this with a variety of short stories and picture books will teach students that different story elements, developed differently, will hook readers for different reasons and in different ways.
2. *Visit* **by Walter Dean Myers—What's the Hook? Lesson** (See Figure 10 on page 42 for lesson plan.)
3. **The Text Engagement Conversation and Reading Log Entries (ongoing).** It is no exaggeration to say that most of our academic goals would be met if we could just find some magic potion that would make students engage meaningfully with what they are reading. And yet, meaningful textual engagement remains as stubbornly elusive as the potion that would precipitate it. We surely do try, though. We offer strategies for engagement (asking questions, making

Grade Level: 6–12   **Lesson Duration:** 2+ class periods

Essential Understanding: The development of individual story elements hooks readers.

Learning Outcomes: Students will know and be able to identify which specific story elements are developed by the author to hook readers.

AASL Standards for the 21st Century Learner:
4.1.2—Read widely and fluently to make connections with self, the world, and previous reading.

	Procedure	Resources
Mini Lesson	Revisit the definitions of each of the story elements: • Pace • Tone • Story Line • Characters/Characterization Explain: Successful authors develop select story elements to hook their readers. Different readers are hooked by different story elements depending on how each of these is developed.	
Guided Practice	Read aloud: *Olivia* by Ian Falconer. Elicit from and discuss with the students: • Which of the story elements are least developed? (Story line and pace are minimally developed.) • Which of the story elements are well developed? (Characterization and tone are fully developed.) • To summarize: There really isn't a "story" here. *Olivia* is all about the character and the humorous way in which the author tells us about her. • What hooks the reader? Identify the hooks: strong characterization and a humorous tone.	*Olivia* by Ian Falconer
Independent Practice	In pairs, students read a variety of picture books and identify the stories' hooks (which of the books' story elements are best developed by their authors). For each book they read, students record (on loose-leaf paper) the title and author and identify the hook(s). Some book suggestions: • *Earrings!* by Judith Viorst • *Paper Boy* by Dav Pilkey • *Coming On Home Soon* by Jacqueline Woodson • *The Day I Swapped My Dad for Two Goldfish* by Neil Gaiman • *The Heart and the Bottle* by Oliver Jeffers	A variety of picture books Loose-leaf paper and pens
Sharing/ Reflection	Elicit: • Which were the stories with the best-developed characters? Explain. • Which were the stories with the best-developed tone? Explain.	

	• Which were the stories with the best-developed pace? Explain. • Which were the stories with the best-developed story lines? Explain.	
Assessment: Collect student papers and review.		

Follow-Up/Extension: Define and describe specific techniques used by authors to develop each of the story elements.

Figure 9.   What's the Hook? Lesson

predictions, monitoring comprehension, and the like). We model and teach the making of a variety of connections (text to self, text to world, text to text).

In point of fact, our overzealousness in this area often leads to precisely the kind of reading we are trying to avoid: interrupted. At every turn, we pause to force connections, predictions, and questioning, and our students dutifully (if only robotically) oblige us. Post-It–littered books, however, are not necessarily proof that our students have engaged with their reading. We strive for deep connections and get superficial ones (what other kind of connection could possibly fit on a Post-It?). We hope for deep thought and get shallow, grade-driven assignment completion. How will we ever break free of this Sisyphean cycle? By teaching our students how to think about and tell us what would engage them without outside coercion and by helping our students find books with which they cannot help but engage—books they fall into and do not want to escape—books they are hooked by. In order for this to happen, however, everyone involved will have to work hard. And while there is no potion, there is a prescription of sorts.

The prescription starts with us. We are the ones to motivate our students to want to find the books that will engage them. We walk the true reader's walk by being honest about our reading likes and dislikes and by allowing our students the same reading luxuries we afford ourselves. We cannot sugar-coat the truth: We figured out what we like to read by reading a whole bunch of stuff we didn't particularly care for as well as reading a whole bunch of stuff we loved. Now we know what to avoid and what to select. It was a learning, reading, and *thinking* process. It did not come to us in a dream, nor was it encoded in our DNA at conception. No one else did it for us. We had to work to discover our preferences, and a large part of that work was allowing ourselves to be deeply enough engaged by our reading to be able to make a sensible determination about whether it spoke to us. There is no way around the idea that we had to *think* about our reading in order to learn about our preferences.

Our students are the critical element. We cannot do this work for them. They surely have the larger stake in the claim of their own reading than we do. Therefore, the lion's share of the work in figuring out their reading preferences will be theirs. Fortunately, there is plenty of material available for them to read that will not consume vast amounts of their time. Picture books and short stories are an ideal starting place because they do not take long to read and have all the same story elements as longer works. As part of an ongoing process of

Grade Level: 8–12   **Lesson Duration:** 1 class period

Essential Question: What hooks readers into Walter Dean Myers's short story *Visit*?

Learning Outcomes: The students will know and be able to identify the hooks for Walter Dean Myers's short story, *Visit*.

AASL Standards for the 21st Century Learner:
4.1.3—Respond to literature and creative expressions of ideas in various formats and genres.

	Procedure	Resources
Mini Lesson	Briefly revisit the definitions of each of the story elements: • Pace • Tone • Story Line • Characters/Characterization Review: Successful authors develop select story elements to hook their readers. Different readers are hooked by different story elements depending on how each of these is developed.	
Guided Practice	Read aloud (as students read along, if possible) *Visit* by Walter Dean Myers. Elicit: • What is the overall feel of this story? Why? • Which of the story elements are best developed in the story? (Tone and pace.) Explain why. • Assign appeal terms to the tone (heavy, quiet, sad) and pace (measured, deliberate). Discuss.	*Visit* by Walter Dean Myers in the short story anthology *Necessary Noise*
Independent Practice	On loose-leaf paper (with a partner), students provide as many synonyms and/or phrases as possible that describe the tone and pace of the story. Have students include how they felt as they read the story. Finally, have them explain why they think someone might be hooked into this story by its tone and pace.	Loose-leaf paper
Sharing/ Reflection	Discuss: • Were you hooked by this story? Why or why not? (Explain: Sometimes, the very thing that makes us dislike a story will make someone else love it—that is its hook.) • What did the author do well? (Develop the tone and pace in such a way as to make the reader feel trapped in the story with the characters.)	
Assessment: Collect Independent Practice and review.		

Follow-Up/Extension: What did you learn about your reading preferences from identifying the hook (s) of *Visit* by Walter Dean Myers?

Figure 10.   *Visit* What's the Hook Lesson

learning about their reading preferences, students should keep a simple log of their picture book and short story reading. Entries in the log should include the items listed in Figure 11.

The expectation is that our students will make the effort to learn one thing about their personal reading preferences from everything they read. In this way, after they have read a number of short stories and picture books, a snapshot of their likes and dislikes should begin to emerge. As with any other expectation we have, it helps to model the process. Even if you already know your preferences, students will benefit from your reading and responding to several picture books and short stories using the Reading Log Entry form.

4. **Summarizing (lesson and ongoing).** (See Figure 12a for lesson plan.) In order to be able to write effective Book Hooks, students will have to learn how to write summaries. These summaries, however, will constitute the least significant part of the Book Hooks they write. It is important to start from a place of understanding that summaries (in the strictest sense of the word) do nothing whatsoever to

---

Title:

Author:

Assign appeal terms and/or synonyms of appeal terms to each of the story elements.

Tone:

Pace:

Story Line:

Characters/Characterization:

The following story element(s) were best developed in this story:

The Hook(s) of this story are:

Here's what I learned about my personal reading preferences from this book:

Figure 11.   Reading Log Entries

Grade Level: 6–12   **Lesson Duration:** 2 class periods

Essential Question: What are the characteristics of good story summaries?

Learning Outcomes: The students will know and be able to identify story summaries that are effective.

AASL Standards for the 21st Century Learner:
4.1.3—Respond to literature and creative expressions of ideas in various formats and genres.

	Procedure	Resources
Mini Lesson	Elicit from students: • What is a summary? (Making something shorter without losing its meaning; an abbreviation.) • What makes a good story summary? (It is short; it gives only the main idea; it is a good general overview of what a story is about.)	White board Loose-leaf paper and pens for students
Guided Practice	Display the summary for *But Excuse Me That Is My Book* by Lauren Child. Elicit: • From reading this summary, what do you expect will happen in this story? (List events in order on the white board.) • Read the story aloud to the class. • Was this summary effective? Why?/Why not? (Discuss.) • What were some of the details that were *intentionally* left out of the summary? (List these on the white board.) • Why were they left out? Discuss. Elicit an *ineffective* summary for the book from the students. Be sure to include too many details from the story and discuss what makes the summary ineffective. Compare it to the one in the book (located on the back of the title page).	*But Excuse Me That Is My Book* by Lauren Child
Independent Practice	Each pair of students repeats the activity above using the Summary Evaluation Worksheet (Figure 12b) and an additional picture book.	A selection of picture books with summaries
Sharing/ Reflection	What did you discover about good summaries? What do you think will be hardest about writing good summaries? Why?	
Assessment: Collect Summary Evaluation Worksheets. Review.		

Follow-Up: Provide students with a number of effective and ineffective summaries to evaluate.
****Extension:** Students read picture books and write summaries for them.

Figure 12a.   Summarizing Lesson

convey the true experience of having read any given story. At best, they convey what the story was *about*. What they do not reveal is what makes the story work. Nor do they shed any light whatsoever on the appeal of a story—unless we make them do so by interweaving appeal throughout the summary. In any event, to start, students will have to learn how to summarize stories.

Title: _____

Author: _____

Summary: _____
_____
_____
_____

From reading only the summary, say what you expect will happen in this story:
_____
_____
_____
_____

Read the story, then evaluate the summary by answering the questions below.
Was this summary effective? Why?/Why not? _____
_____
_____
_____
_____
_____

List some of the details that were *intentionally* left out of the summary.
_____
_____
_____
_____

Write a slightly different but equally effective summary for this story.

Figure 12b.   Summary Evaluation Worksheet

Summary writing is an art form. The best summaries are concise distillations that reveal only the most salient points of a piece of writing. Unfortunately, the tendency most students have is to oversummarize. Rather than distilling what they have read down to several sentences, they tend to produce summaries that are too often longer than the original piece of writing they were asked to summarize. Clearly, this happens because they are unable to distinguish between what is pertinent and what is less relevant to the task of conveying the meat of any given story. They get stuck on the minutia and feel compelled to include all of it in their summaries.

We can teach lessons on summarizing until we are blue in the face. The reality is that unless students practice summarizing on a regular basis, they will never master it. Part of that same reality is that they need us to repeatedly model the activity for them. The good news is that most teachers acknowledge this is a skill their students would greatly benefit from learning (it is, after all, a direct lead-in to main idea and supporting details work). As such, suggesting they learn to do so in the service of writing good Book Hooks should not require all that much convincing.

Once again, picture books come to the rescue. The fact that each of them has a summary on the back of its title page will come in tremendously handy to begin teaching the skill of summarizing to students. Additionally, using these summaries can stand in as a form of modeling. Finally, once students have internalized the features of good summaries, evaluated a number of summaries, and practiced doing so with a variety of picture books, they can begin to write their own summaries for picture books (without reading the ones provided in the books ahead of time).

Finally, return to *Visit* by Walter Dean Myers. Provided not too much time has elapsed since the earlier lesson using the story, do not reread it with the students, as this will immediately fill their heads with details they will feel compelled to include in a summary. Remind the students of the features of effective summaries and elicit from them what they remember the story to be about. Next, work with them to distill the story down to its barest-bones summary: A father visits his son on death row. Be sure to point out that the titles of stories sometimes provide readers with a good sense of what they will broadly be about. In the case of this story, such is precisely the case. Clearly, however, this story is about much more than just a visit, and this is the point you will want to keep iterating with your students to move them from simple summary into Book Hook writing. Move directly into the next activities.

5. **Building a Book Hook.** If the leap from summary to Book Hook seems daunting, it may help to think of it in terms of building. Think of the summary as the frame of the Book Hook. A story's hook(s) and its appeal build out the structure. (See Figure 13a on page 47 for lesson plan.)

Loosely, the steps to building a strong Book Hook are:

- Read and summarize the story.
- Identify what the story is *really* about.
- Reread to identify hooks and assign appeal.
- Weave appeal, special features, and what the story is really about throughout the summary.
- Close by using the language of appeal to provide an overall snapshot.

The **Building a Book Hook Form** (Figure 13b on page 48; also available as reproducible **A-11 in Appendix A)** can be used as a guide for students. Use the completed one to model how to follow the steps to build a Book Hook for *Visit*. Before doing the latter, however, you will want to build several Book Hooks with your students using picture books. A sample lesson for doing so is included in Figure 13a. Use the same story you used in the Summarizing lesson (in the case of this book: *But Excuse Me That Is My Book* by Lauren Child).

Note: As you model the building of a Book Hook for *Visit* by Walter Dean Myers using the completed form, be sure to elicit as much as you possibly can from your students. (See Figure 14 on page 49 for a sample.)

Grade Level: 6–12   **Lesson Duration:** 2 class periods

Essential Question: How are the elements of a Book Hook used to build one?

Learning Outcomes: The students will know and be able to use the elements of a Book Hook to build one.

AASL Standards for the 21st Century Learner:
4.1.3 Respond to literature and creative expressions of ideas in various formats and genres.

	Procedure	Resources
Mini Lesson	• Project Building a Book Hook form (Figure 13b) on the board. • Elicit from students what they think the difference is between a summary and a Book Hook (the former tells what a story is about, the latter tells what the story's hooks are, what its appeal is, and what the story is really about). • Point out the elements necessary to build a Book Hook (title, author, summary, what the story is really about, hook(s), appeal, special features, and three words or phrases that best describe the book).	Building a Book Hook form (Figure 13b) White board
Guided Practice	• Copy the title and author onto the form. • Read the story *But Excuse Me That Is My Book.* • Elicit a summary of the story and record on the Building a Book Hook form. (If you prefer, use the summary in the book located on the back of the title page.) • Elicit and record what the story is really about. • Elicit the hook(s) (characterization and tone). • Apply appeal terms and synonyms to the hooks (well-developed and well-drawn character, humorous tone). • Identify special features (unique, collage-like illustrations). • Model weaving all of the above into a Book Hook for students. • Identify the three words or phrases that best describe the story (completely character-driven story line, quirky and recognizable main character, humorous tone).	*But Excuse Me That Is My book* by Lauren Child Projected Building a Book Hook form
Independent Practice	• Pairs of students work on completing Building a Book Hook forms using an assortment of picture books to do so.	Multiple Building a Book Hook forms An assortment of picture books
Sharing/ Reflection	• What was the hardest part of completing the Building a Book Hook form? Why? • In what ways does it help to identify each of the elements of a story's Book Hook before actually having to write one?	
Assessment: Collect completed Building a Book Hook forms and review.		

Follow-Up/Extension: Move students from using picture books to using short stories and novels they have read to write Book Hooks.

Figure 13a.   Building a Book Hook Lesson

Building a Book Hook

Title:

Author:

Summary:

What is this story really about?

Identify the hook(s)/best-developed story elements. (Check only the story elements that are best developed by the author—these are the hooks.)

_____ Pace_____ Tone _____ Story Line _____ Characters/Characterization

Restate the best-developed story elements/hooks and assign them appeal terms and synonyms:

Identify any special features of the story here:

Rewrite the summary incorporating the hooks, appeal terms, and any special features.

Three words or phrases that best describe this book are:

Figure 13b.   Building a Book Hook Form

Building a Book Hook

Title: *Visit*

Author: Walter Dean Myers

Summary: A father visits his son on death row.

What is this story really about? It is about all of the emotions a man and his son feel meeting each other for the first time on death row. It is about denial, regret, profound discomfort, sadness, and the inescapability of consequences.

Identify the hook(s)/best-developed story elements. (Check only the story elements that are best developed by the author—these are the hooks.)
 X Pace *X* Tone _____ Story Line _____ Characters/Characterization

Restate the best-developed story elements/hooks and assign them appeal terms and synonyms:

Pace: very deliberate and measured to build discomfort in reader. Time stands still.

Tone: impossibly sad, hopeless, and grim

Identify any special features of the story here:

• The emotional discomfort is as inescapable as the final consequence.

Here's the Hook: Rewrite the summary incorporating the hook(s), appeal terms, and any special features.

Time passes at a painfully measured pace during a father's visit to this estranged son on death row. What drawn-out minutes are left to them are spent in discomfort, confession, regret, and resignation. Hopelessness and the final consequence are inescapable.

Three words or phrases that best describe this story are:
• Grim and impossibly hopeless tone
• Extremely deliberate and measured pace
• Completely emotional story line

Figure 14.   Building a Book Hook for *Visit* by Walter Dean Myers

A Closing Thought

Throughout this book, a number of activities have been suggested (from implementation plans to workshops for colleagues and lessons with students). These activities have been suggested with the full understanding that more often than not, it is a given that obstacles will be encountered at various points in the process of trying to implement a new initiative. Much like trying to get a rocket off the ground, tremendous amounts of energy are required—if only to break free of the gravitational drag created by deeply entrenched resistance to change. A large part of the energy you will find yourself expending (should you decide to undertake the endeavor of teaching appeal terms and Book Hook writing to students) will be directed into developing a persistence of vision so keen as to allow you to forge ahead with your goals despite initial failures and possibly not having every single colleague on board. You may have to start small and gradually build from there. You may be fortunate enough to have full commitment from the outset. You may fall somewhere in between. In any case, there will be mighty work to do. In all cases, what will gratify most is when students begin to discover and systematically share their reading preferences. You will not easily forget the face and name of the first child that walks into your library and asks for a book that has "a fast pace and a dark tone."

Appendix A:
Reproducible Forms

Appendix A-1
The Book Hook (Artwork: Fiona Creed).

GET HOOKED ON READING!!

Title: _____

Author: _____

Genre: _____

Here's the Hook:

_____

_____

_____

_____

_____

_____

Three words or phrases that best describe
this book are:

_____

_____

Name: _____

Class: _____

GET HOOKED ON READING!!

Title: _____

Author: _____

Genre: _____

Here's the Hook:

_____

_____

_____

_____

_____

_____

Three words or phrases that best
describe this book are:

_____

_____

Name: _____

Class: _____

Appendix A-2
Proposal for Administration Worksheet
Appeal Terms and Book Hooks—A Proposal

Using Part I of this book and adding your personal thoughts, pull together the most salient points and materials you will need to make a case to administration for teaching appeal terms concepts and the writing of Book Hooks to your school's students.

A brief definition of appeal terms

Appeal terms are _____

_____

_____

_____

(Attach The Vocabulary of Appeal to this document.)

Three reasons you think your students should be taught appeal terms:

1. _____
2. _____
3. _____

A brief definition of Book Hooks

A Book Hook is: _____

_____

_____

_____

(Attach the blank Book Hook form and a completed sample Book Hook to this document.)

Three reasons you think your students should be taught how to write Book Hooks:

1. _____
2. _____
3. _____

Book Hook Sharing

In order to implement the systematic sharing of Book Hooks, we will need the following supplies in the specified quantities:

_____ three-inch ring binders (one per ELA classroom)

_____ dividers (one per student in each ELA classroom)

_____ copies of Book Hooks (two per page—three per student to start)

_____ plastic sheet protectors (three per student to start)

_____ copies of completed sample Book Hooks for the front of each binder

The library will also need a three-inch ring binder, a set of ten dividers, and a package of sheet protectors.

Here are three ways in which I think the reading culture in our building might be improved by the implementation of appeal terms and Book Hook writing:

1. _____

2. _____

3. _____

Here are three ways in which I envision myself (as the librarian) supporting our school's ELA teachers in this endeavor:

1. _____

2. _____

3. _____

Finally, attach a rough draft of a Book Hook writing and sharing procedure for possible inclusion in the school's Policy and Procedures Manual.

Appendix A-3
Reading Survey

This survey was created by K. Blair and O. Nesi with thanks in part to information consulted from: Saricks, Joyce G. *Readers' Advisory Service in the Public Library*, 3rd Ed. (Chicago: American Library Association, 2005).

Think about books you've read that you've really enjoyed. Keep these books in mind as you complete this survey.

1. What is most important to you in a story? Check only one.

_____the pace at which the story moves

_____the characters

_____the story line (the way the story unfolds)

_____the tone—in other words the general atmosphere created by the book

2. What was the last book you really loved? List two things that you loved most.

3. What was the last book you read that you really disliked? List two things that you disliked most.

Pacing
I **prefer** stories that are (check only one):

_____leisurely paced, unhurried, and relaxed.

_____fast paced.

Characterization
I **prefer** characters that are (check only one):

_____realistic, recognizable, relatable, and familiar.

_____unique, eccentric, and quirky.

_____thoughtful and self-aware.

Story Line
I **prefer** stories that (check only one):

_____have a character-centered, interior, or psychological approach.

_____are centered on events and plot.

_____have unexpected story lines and plot twists and turns.

Atmosphere/Tone: The feel of a novel
I **prefer** stories that have a (check only one):

_____scary, foreboding, and ominous tone.

_____heartwarming and touching tone.

_____comic, funny, and upbeat tone.

_____sad and depressing tone.

_____suspenseful, nerve-wracking tone.

Questions to consider. Check either yes or no—not both.

Question	Yes	No
• I like books with more dialogue than description/inner thoughts		
• I like books with short sentences and/ or short paragraphs.		
• I like books with short chapters.		
• I like stories that focus on one character.		
• I like stories that focus on multiple characters whose lives are intertwined.		
• I like stories that are told from one narrator's point of view.		
• I like stories told from multiple points of view.		
• I like secondary characters that impact a story.		
• I like stories that emphasize characters.		
• I like stories that focus on situations and events.		
• I like stories that are dramatic and dark.		
• I like stories that are inviting and cozy.		
• I like stories that are edgy and agitated.		

Appendix A-4

Summary vs. Appeal Terms

Write a brief summary or annotation for the last two novels you read.

Book Title and Author #1: _____
A brief summary:

Book Title and Author #2: _____
A brief summary:

Revisit each of the titles and describe them using the appeal terms provided below. (Circle all that apply and/or add your own.)

Book #1
The pace is: breakneck engrossing relaxed unhurried other: _____

The characters are (or characterization is): familiar multiple points of view quirky realistic well developed other: _____

The story line is: action oriented character centered violent gentle open-ended thought-provoking tragic other: _____

The atmosphere/tone is: dark edgy hard-edged humorous magical romantic suspenseful other: _____

Book #2
The pace is: breakneck engrossing relaxed unhurried other: _____

The characters are (or characterization is): familiar multiple points of view quirky realistic well developed other: _____

The story line is: action oriented character centered violent gentle open-ended thought-provoking tragic other: _____

The atmosphere/tone is: dark edgy hard-edged humorous magical romantic suspenseful other: _____

Revisit each of the titles again, and this time, rewrite each of the summaries from above, incorporating the appeal terms you selected for each of the books.

Appendix A-5

Appeal Terms Worksheet (Modified from: *Readers' Advisory Service in the Public Library* by Joyce Saricks [3rd ed. Chicago: ALA, 2005])

Title: _____

Author (Last, First): _____

Story Element—Pace

☐ breakneck	☐ compelling	☐ deliberate
☐ densely written	☐ easy	☐ engrossing
☐ fast	☐ leisurely	☐ lively
☐ measured	☐ relaxed	☐ stately
☐ unhurried		

Story Element—Tone

☐ bittersweet	☐ bleak	☐ contemporary
☐ creepy	☐ dark	☐ detailed setting
☐ edgy	☐ engaging	☐ exotic
☐ foreboding	☐ gritty	☐ hard edged
☐ heartwarming	☐ heavy	☐ hopeful
☐ humorous	☐ lush	☐ magical
☐ melodramatic	☐ menacing	☐ mystical
☐ nightmare	☐ political	☐ psychological
☐ quiet	☐ romantic	☐ sad
☐ spooky	☐ stark	☐ suspenseful
☐ timeless	☐ upbeat	

Story Element—Story Line

☐ action oriented	☐ character centered	☐ complex
☐ domestic	☐ episodic	☐ event oriented
☐ fact filled	☐ family centered	☐ gentle
☐ inspirational	☐ issue oriented	☐ layered
☐ multiple plotlines	☐ mystical	☐ mythic
☐ open ended	☐ plot centered	☐ plot twists
☐ resolved ending	☐ rich and famous	☐ setting oriented
☐ thought provoking	☐ tragic	☐ violent

Story Element—Characters/Characterization

☐ detailed	☐ distant	☐ dramatic
☐ eccentric	☐ evocative	☐ faithful
☐ familiar	☐ intriguing secondary characters	☐ introspective
☐ lifelike	☐ multiple point of view	☐ quirky
☐ realistic	☐ recognizable	☐ series characters
☐ vivid	☐ well developed	☐ well drawn

The special feature (s) of this book are: _____

_____

_____

_____

_____

_____

_____

Appendix A-6
Book Hook Worksheet
GET HOOKED ON READING!

Title: _____

Author: _____

Genre: _____

Circle the adjectives that best describe the various appeal terms of your book:

The pace is: breakneck engrossing fast relaxed unhurried

other: _____

The characters are (or the characterization is): familiar multiple points of view quirky realistic well developed **other:** _____

The story line is: action oriented character centered violent gentle open ended Thought provoking tragic **other:** _____

The atmosphere/tone is: dark edgy hard-edged humorous magical romantic suspenseful **other:** _____

The special feature(s) of this book is (are): _____

_____

_____

_____

_____

Appendix A-7

So, What Is a Book Hook and How Do I Write One?

What Is a Book Hook Exactly?

- A pitch of sorts
- Neither a plot summary nor a book review
- More like a blurb than either a plot summary or a book review
- Should capture the elements of a book in such a way as to entice someone to want to read it
- Gives readers an "in" to the book by revealing its hook
- Because different readers are hooked by different elements, Book Hooks on the same book written by different writers will be different.

. . . and How Do I Write One?

- Begin by referring to the list of appeal terms as you read.
- Jot down the adjectives you think best describe the feel of the book you are reading.
- Include as little as possible about the plot.
- Determine which of the story elements to feature in your Book Hook, then work them in.
- Practice, practice, practice (and it helps if you like the book).

Appendix A-8
Plot-Based Descriptions vs. Book Hooks

Title: *Unwind* by Neal Shusterman

Plot-Based Description:

Three teens are attempting to escape from a society that salvages body parts from children ages thirteen to eighteen.

Book Hook (O. Nesi):
Unwinding: a procedure in which the bodies of unwanted kids between the ages of thirteen and eighteen are taken apart piece by piece and harvested for use by others.

In a world gone absolutely mad, Connor, Lev, and Risa are running for their lives—desperate to escape being unwound. By turns frantic, angry, fearful, and hopeless, the teens' fight for their lives is full of white-knuckled tension, page-turning suspense, and dizzying action.

Title: *Remembering Raquel* by Vivian Vande Velde

Plot-Based Description:
When Raquel is killed in a car accident, the woman responsible for her death, her friends, classmates, and family members reflect on her life and how her death has impacted their lives.

Book Hook (O. Nesi):
How did fourteen-year-old Raquel Falcone die? Was she accidentally or intentionally pushed in front of an oncoming car? Did she lose her footing and fall down under it? Or did she step in front of it on purpose? Told from the points of view of the people in her life, this quick read is full of small plot shifts and surprising plot twists, each packing a major emotional punch.

Title: *Acceleration* by Graham McNamee

Plot-Based Description:
Seventeen-year-old Duncan is stuck working in the lost-and-found department of the Toronto Transit Authority when he comes across the diary of a serial killer and decides to stop him.

Book Hook (O. Nesi):
Duncan's summer job in the subway's lost and found seems like it's going to be a total bore—until he comes across the diary of a serial killer. Prepare for a rollercoaster ride of creepiness and nail-biting suspense as Duncan and his friends try to track the psycho down before he graduates from torturing and killing animals to torturing and killing people. Alternating between "guy" humor and disturbing glimpses into a twisted mind, this book is completely gripping—a true adrenaline-fueled rocket ride.

From *Getting Beyond "Interesting": Teaching Students the Vocabulary of Appeal to Discuss Their Reading* by Olga M. Nesi. Santa Barbara, CA: Libraries Unlimited. Copyright © 2012.

Appendix A-9
Book Hook Rubric

Category	4	3	2	1	Points Earned
The Hook	The Hook is extremely persuasive. Any summarizing present is minimal and used only to promote the book.	The Hook is somewhat persuasive. There is more summarizing than is necessary to promote the book	The Hook is mostly summary, with minimal persuasion.	The Hook is all summary and not at all persuasive	
Appeal Terms	All three appeal terms used support the Hook and show originality.	Two of the three appeal terms used support the Hook and show originality.	One of the three appeal terms used supports the Hook and shows originality.	No appeal terms are used.	
Grammar	There are no grammatical or spelling mistakes on the Book Hook.	There is one grammatical or spelling mistake on the Book Hook.	There are two to three grammatical or spelling mistakes on the Book Hook.	There are more than three grammatical or spelling mistakes on the Book Hook.	
Neatness and Effort	The Book Hook has no distracting errors, corrections, or erasures and is easily read. It appears the student spent a lot of effort getting things just right.	The Book Hook has almost no distracting errors, corrections, or erasures and is easily read. It appears the student worked hard on it.	The Book Hook is fairly readable, but the quality is not too good on some parts. It looks like the student ran out of time or didn't take care of it.	The Book Hook is very messy and hard to read. It looks like the student threw it together at the last minute without much care.	

From: Getting Beyond Interesting...

Appendix A-10
Appeal Bookmarks

Appeal Terms Bookmark Title/Author: Your Name:	Appeal Terms Bookmark Title/Author: Your Name:	Appeal Terms Bookmark Title/Author: Your Name:
What's the PACE?	**What's the PACE?**	**What's the PACE?**
☐ leisurely/relaxed	☐ leisurely/relaxed	☐ leisurely/relaxed
☐ lively	☐ lively	☐ lively
☐ fast	☐ fast	☐ fast
☐ breakneck	☐ breakneck	☐ breakneck
☐ engrossing	☐ engrossing	☐ engrossing
What's the TONE?	**What's the TONE?**	**What's the TONE?**
☐ bittersweet	☐ bittersweet	☐ bittersweet
☐ heartwarming/hopeful/ upbeat	☐ heartwarming/hopeful/ upbeat	☐ heartwarming/hopeful/ upbeat
☐ humorous	☐ humorous	☐ humorous
☐ magical	☐ magical	☐ magical
☐ creepy/spooky	☐ creepy/spooky	☐ creepy/spooky
☐ dark/edgy	☐ dark/edgy	☐ dark/edgy
☐ heavy/sad	☐ heavy/sad	☐ heavy/sad
☐ suspenseful	☐ suspenseful	☐ suspenseful
☐ melodramatic	☐ melodramatic	☐ melodramatic
What's the STORY LINE?	**What's the STORY LINE?**	**What's the STORY LINE?**
☐ action oriented	☐ action oriented	☐ action oriented
☐ character centered	☐ character centered	☐ character centered
☐ gentle	☐ gentle	☐ gentle
☐ open ended	☐ open ended	☐ open ended
☐ thought provoking	☐ thought provoking	☐ thought provoking
☐ tragic	☐ tragic	☐ tragic
☐ violent	☐ violent	☐ violent
What's the CHARACTERIZATION?	**What's the CHARACTERIZATION?**	**What's the CHARACTERIZATION?**
☐ familiar/realistic/lifelike	☐ familiar/realistic/lifelike	☐ familiar/realistic/lifelike
☐ multiple points of view	☐ multiple points of view	☐ multiple points of view
☐ quirky	☐ quirky	☐ quirky
☐ vivid/well developed	☐ vivid/well developed	☐ vivid/well developed

Appendix B: Resources

Appendix B-1
Student Appeal List

Books That Hooked Us With Their Appeal

Be sure to refer to the library catalog for brief plot summaries of any of the books that seem like they might appeal to you.

Begging for Change **by Sharon Flake. Genre: Realistic Fiction/Problem Novel**
Hajar S. (Class 806) and Zsanet L. (Class 8-149) say three words or phrases that best describe this book are: "bittersweet tone, vivid characters, inspiring story line."

Exit Point **by Laura Langston. Genre: Magical Realism**
Tarell B. (Class 808) says three words or phrases that best describe this book are: "this book puts you right into the story, tense tone, very thought-provoking story line."

Hero **by S. L. Rottman. Genre: Realistic Fiction/Problem Novel**
Kai L. (Class 802) says three words or phrases that best describe this book are: "bittersweet tone, powerfully thought-provoking story line, lifelike characters."

The Kite Runner **by Khaled Hosseini. Genre: Realistic Fiction**
Aaisha J. (Class 802) says three words or phrases that best describe this book are: "compelling pace, touching, and extremely emotional story line."

Life As We Knew It **by Susan Beth Pfeffer. Genre: Science Fiction**
Inna M. (Class 805) says three words or phrases that best describe this book are: "suspenseful tone, well-developed characters, captivating story line."

Perfect **by Natasha Friend. Genre: Realistic Fiction/Problem Novel**
Heena A. (Class 806) says three words or phrases that best describe this book are: "measured pace, lifelike situations, recognizable characters."

Queen of the Toilet Bowl **by Frieda Wishinsky. Genre: Realistic Fiction/Problem Novel**
Cansu Z. (Class 806) says three words or phrases that best describe this book are: "uncomfortable real-life situations, plot twists, anxious/tense tone."

***Slam* by Nick Hornby. Genre: Humorous Realistic Fiction**
Anthony A. (Class 810) says three words or phrases that best describe this book are: "fast paced, humorous tone, realistic situations."

***Tunnels* by Gordon Roderick. Genre: Fantasy/Action Adventure**
Igor Z. (Class 809) says three words or phrases that best describe this book are: "mysterious tone, action-packed story line, rollercoaster ride."

Appendix B-2
Library Book Hooks List #1

If you like books with a **dark tone** and a **suspenseful story line**, try these titles:

The Black Book of Secrets by F. E. Higgins. **Genre: Fantasy**
Here's the Hook: From its nail-bitingly tense opening scene to its magical conclusion, this book takes hold and never lets go for an instant. Enter the life of young Ludlow Fitch as he becomes the apprentice of Joe Zabbidou, Secret Pawnbroker. Hear the dark confessions of the gravedigger, the butcher, and the book and coffin makers—each whispered at midnight to Joe in the back room of his pawnshop in the town of Pagus Parvus and recorded by Ludlow in *The Black Book of Secrets*. And what of Jeremiah Ratchet, the greedy, greasy landlord of many of the townspeople of Pagus Parvus? In this gripping tale, all is revealed in due and proper time.

The Compound by S. A. Bodeen. **Genre: Science Fiction**
Here's the Hook: In this dark, disturbing novel, you are trapped underground with Eli and the Yanakakis family. The compound they live in is huge and was well stocked. They escaped into it following what their father told them was a nuclear war. Six years later, food is running out and the behaviors of Eli and his sisters are getting weirder and weirder. But if their actions are strange, that's nothing compared to those of their father. How long could you live underground without ever being able to leave? What if you suspected you *could* leave, but your father was preventing you from doing so?

Deep and Dark and Dangerous by Mary Downing Hahn. **Genre: Ghost Story**
Here's the Hook: Sycamore Lake is deep, dark, and dangerous. The weather in Maine is cold, rainy, and gloomy, and the family cabin is surrounded by trees and, often, fog. Ali vacations at the cabin in the hope of getting an answer to her questions: Who was the third girl in that picture of her mom and her Aunt Dulcie and why was she torn out of the photograph? What, exactly, happened at the lake some thirty years earlier that made the family abandon the cabin? Why does her four-year-old cousin Emma keep dreaming about bones in the lake, and why does Ali keep getting the feeling that something is lurking in the dark corners of the cabin?

Eye of the Crow by Shane Peacock. **Genre: Historical Fiction/Mystery**
Here's the Hook: A beautiful young woman is found murdered in the back alley of a London slum in the year 1867. A young butcher's assistant is arrested for the crime and set to hang for it as well. Thirteen-year-old Sherlock Holmes knows the murder was committed by someone else entirely. Feel the thrill of sneaking with Sherlock into the homes of those he suspects of having committed the murder. Follow Sherlock into the dark, twisting, suffocating alleys of London as he solves his first case.

Hurricane Song by Paul Volponi. **Genre: Realistic Fiction**
Here's the Hook: In this bleak account of the aftereffects of Hurricane Katrina, readers are trapped with Miles and his father in the sweltering, stench-ridden Super Dome in New

Orleans. Adding further to the pain and sadness of the story is the fact that Miles and his father do not get along. Miles cannot shake the feeling that his dad loves his jazz music far more than he loves him. Gradually, a picture of human suffering, racial tensions, and unspeakably awful behavior is painted. The only thing rising above the horror of the situation is the human ability to hope in the face of despair.

Martyn Pig by Kevin Brooks. **Genre: Realistic Fiction/Problem Novel**
Here's the Hook: In this dark, bleak, and heavy novel, Martyn Pig kills his alcoholic and abusive father in self-defense. Afraid to call the police, he lives with the body in the filthy, squalid, rancid house for four days. In this time, he descends into numbness and emptiness, eventually surrendering to fate and ultimately coming up with a plan to dispose of the body. In a completely breathtaking plot twist, he discovers the true meaning of evil.

The Rules of Survival by Nancy Werlin. **Genre: Realistic Fiction/Problem Novel**
Here's the Hook: Matt is thirteen, Callie is eleven, and Emmy is five. All three of their lives are a rollercoaster ride of physical and emotional abuse at the hands of their mother, Nikki. Struggling to survive, they develop coping strategies to deal with their mother's unpredictable personality, drug use, and episodes of hair-raising violence.

The Seer of Shadows by Avi. **Genre: Historical Fiction/Mystery**
Here's the Hook: The year is 1872 and fourteen-year-old Horace Carpentine is apprenticed to a photographer in New York City. Little does he know that he will soon discover a special talent he has for creating living ghosts through the process of taking and developing photographs. Join him on his spine-tingling, hair-raising adventures as he gives "life" once again to a dead, abused little girl named Eleanora. In this gripping tale of ghostly vengeance, the pages keep turning—nearly outside of your own power.

Twisted by Laurie Halse Anderson. **Genre: Realistic Fiction/Problem Novel**
Here's the Hook: Tyler Miller is invisible to everyone but his angry, miserable father and an assortment of bullies at school until a graffiti stunt lands him in hard labor for the summer and gains him both a criminal reputation and the attention of girls. When his life starts to spiral out of control, Tyler realizes he has difficult and painful choices to make. He will either transform himself or remain trapped in others' perceptions of him.

Unwind by Neal Schusterman. **Genre: Science Fiction**
Here's the Hook: Unwinding: a procedure in which the bodies of unwanted kids between the ages of thirteen and eighteen are taken apart piece by piece and harvested for use by others. In a world gone absolutely mad, Connor, Lev, and Risa are running for their lives, desperate to escape being unwound. By turns frantic, angry, fearful, and hopeless, the teens' fight for their lives is full of white-knuckled tension, page-turning suspense, and dizzying action.

Appendix B-3
Library Book Hooks List #2

If you like books with lots of **action** and a **fast pace**, try these titles:

How Angel Peterson Got His Name by Gary Paulsen. Genre: Humorous Memoir
Here's the Hook: In a whirlwind of nonstop, hair-raising action, Gary Paulsen takes readers back to his boyhood in Minnesota in the late 1940s. "Boys will be boys" no matter what the year, so make way for Paulsen and his friends to entertain you with unbelievable stories of the variety of insane stunts that nearly got them killed at the age of thirteen. A small sampling includes: being pulled on skis by a car going seventy-four miles per hour, jumping a bike through a hoop of fire, wrestling a bear, and hang gliding with an army surplus kite. Be amazed—but whatever you do, don't try these stunts at home!

Knucklehead: Tall Tales & Mostly True Stories About Growing Up Scieszka by John Scieszka. Genre: Humorous Memoir
Here's the Hook: In this humorous memoir, the author of *The Stinky Cheese Man and Other Fairly Stupid Fairy Tales* recounts his childhood growing up with five brothers. No sooner does one of the brothers get his collarbone broken playing football than another one is tied to his bed and yet another digs up the houseplants and eats the dirt. Chock full of surprises and knuckleheaded behavior, this memoir creates a vivid picture of nonstop boy action as Jon Scieszka and his brothers run wild, wreck and throw things, and cause constant chaos for Mom and Dad.

The Last Apprentice by John Delaney. Genre: Fantasy
Here's the Hook: As the seventh son of a seventh son, Thomas Ward is the last hope of the county. For years, Old Gregory has been the county's Spook, ridding the local villages of evil (capturing witches, binding boggarts, and driving away ghosts). It is time for him to retire. Someone will have to take over his job. Twenty-nine apprentices have tried. Some were too frightened, some fled, some died trying. Thomas is the last apprentice to undertake facing down spine-chilling evil in Chipenden County.

Lawn Boy by Gary Paulsen. Genre: Humorous Realistic Fiction
Here's the Hook: How much money do you figure you could make if your loopy grandmother gave you an old riding lawnmower for your birthday? Enough to buy an inner tube for your old ten-speed bike? Would you make fifty dollars? Two hundred dollars? Eight thousand dollars? How about fifty thousand dollars? In this hilarious little book, one twist leads to another, and a twelve-year-old suddenly finds himself involved in way more than he anticipated.

The Name of This Book Is Secret by Pseudonymous Bosch. Genre: Mystery, Action/Adventure
Here's the Hook: "This is a story *about* a secret. But it's also a *secret* story." (Bosch, 5) You know how secrets are—don't you? Go ahead, just try to make believe you don't want to

know the secret. And if you really don't want to know, then just don't read this book—I dare you! But if you do want to know the secret, pick up this action-packed, riddle, puzzle- and code-filled book and settle in for a zooming, twisting ride through a story of magic and mystery. Surprises await you at every turn.

Appendix B-4
What Should I Read Next? Why?

Directions: Here you will find brief summaries for five books I enjoyed reading. They are arranged in the order in which I read them. Review the information, then reflect on the questions at the end.

1. *Stiff: The Curious Lives of Human Cadavers* **by Mary Roach.** Throughout history, human cadavers have been used in a number of ways to greatly benefit just about every aspect of human existence. This book is an exploration of the ways in which dead bodies have advanced humankind's knowledge.
2. *The Art of Eating* **by MFK Fisher.** An anthology of essays on a variety of culinary topics by food writer MFK Fisher.
3. *Low Life: Lures and Snares of Old New York* **by Luc Sante.** The dark side of Manhattan from approximately 1840 to 1919 is explored. Includes (but is not limited to) the following topics: crooked cops, street urchins, prostitution, city government, and popular entertainment.
4. *An Anthropologist on Mars* **by Oliver Sacks.** The individual worlds and new perspectives of neurological patients are revealed through this collection of their particular histories and their personal departures from neurological normalcy.
5. *Naked* **by David Sedaris.** National Public Radio commentator David Sedaris presents a collection of humorous autobiographical essays in which he discusses (among other topics) a stay at a nudist colony, odd jobs, strange relationships, and his nervous tic.

Questions to Ponder:

- Given the information presented here, what questions would you ask me to try to ascertain what my reading preferences are?
- Alternatively, if you think you know what my reading preferences are, how do you know?
- What would you recommend I read next? Why?

Appendix B-5
Picture Book Bibliography Alphabetical by Title

Pace: lively **Tone:** engaging/humorous **Story Line:** thought provoking* **Characters:** quirky   1. *A Bad Case of the Stripes* by David Shannon. Desperate to be liked by everyone, Camilla Cream becomes the very embodiment of everyone else's wishes—until the day she finally learns to be herself. Genre: magical realism
Pace: unhurried **Tone:** bittersweet/heartwarming **Story Line:** fact filled* **Characters:** vivid   2. *A Band of Angels—A Story Inspired by the Jubilee Singers* by Deborah Hopkinson. The gospel group Jubilee Singers is formed by the daughter of a slave to try to raise money to save Fiske School—a school established in 1866 and dedicated to the education of freed slaves. Includes historical notes at the end. Genre: nonfiction
Pace: compelling **Tone:** timeless*/bittersweet **Story Line:** episodic **Characters:** introspective/quirky*   3. *A Blue So Blue* by Jean-Francois Dumont. A little boy who loves to paint goes in search of the perfect and exact shade of blue of his dreams. His search takes him full circle back to the blue of his mother's eyes. Genre: allegory
Pace: deliberate* **Tone:** hopeful*/heartwarming **Story Line:** event oriented (saving to buy a chair)/ family centered/domestic **Characters:** lifelike   4. *A Chair for My Mother* by Vera B. Williams. Following a fire that destroyed all their furniture, a little girl, her mother, and her grandmother save to buy a comfortable chair. Genre: realistic
Pace: unhurried **Tone:** quiet/sad/heavy* **Story Line:** issue oriented/family centered **Characters:** realistic   5. *A Day's Work* by Eve Bunting. In search of day work for his newly arrived grandfather, Francisco lies and ends up having to learn a difficult but essential lesson from his abuelo. Genre: realistic
Pace: measured **Tone:** timeless* **Story Line:** thought provoking **Characters:** n/a   6. *A Gift From the Sea* by Kate Banks. A young boy finds a rock at the beach but cannot possibly know its long history or all the places it has been over the millennia before it washed up on the shore. Genre: natural science
Pace: deliberate **Tone:** suspenseful **Story Line:** thought provoking*/issue oriented **Characters:** lifelike   7. *A Good Night for Freedom* by Barbara Olenyk Morrow. Upon discovering two runaway slave girls in her neighbor's cellar, Hallie must decide if she will meddle in the affair (against her father's wishes) or maintain neutrality (as her father urges her to do). Genre: historical
Pace: lively **Tone:** bittersweet **Story Line:** resolved ending **Characters:** n/a   8. *A Mama for Owen* by Marion Dane Bauer. Based on the true story of a baby hippo (Owen) separated from its mother and befriending a tortoise named Mzee. Includes factual notes about the story at the end. Genre: nonfiction
Pace: relaxed **Tone:** upbeat **Story Line:** family centered **Characters:** recognizable   9. *A Picnic in October* by Eve Bunting. A young boy finally understands the significance of his family going for a picnic on Liberty Island each year in October. Genre: realistic
Pace: deliberate **Tone:** sad/bleak*/suspenseful **Story Line:** issue oriented **Characters:** quirky   10. *Almost to Freedom* by Vaunda Micheaux Nelson. The story of a slave family's escape from a Southern plantation is told from the viewpoint of the rag doll belonging to the little girl in the family. Genre: historical
Pace: unhurried **Tone:** bittersweet/hopeful* **Story Line:** character centered **Characters:** realistic   11. *Amelia's Road* by Linda Jacobs Altman. As the child of migrant farm workers, Amelia tires of constantly traveling from one farm to another and longs to find a permanent home. Genre: realistic

 From *Getting Beyond "Interesting": Teaching Students the Vocabulary of Appeal to Discuss Their Reading* by Olga M. Nesi. Santa Barbara, CA: Libraries Unlimited. Copyright © 2012.

Pace: engrossing **Tone:** bittersweet* **Story Line:** gentle **Characters:** quirky

12. *Amos and Boris* by William Steig. Amos the mouse and Boris the whale become friends as each saves the other's life. Think: Aesop's fable of the lion and the mouse. Genre: fable

Pace: easy **Tone:** engaging **Story Line:** resolved ending **Characters:** dramatic

13. *Anansi the Spider* by Gerald McDermott. Anansi's seven sons use each of their special talents to rescue him from trouble. Genre: folktale

Pace: unhurried **Tone:** bittersweet/hopeful **Story Line:** family centered* **Characters:** realistic

14. *Angel Child, Dragon Child* by Michele Maria Surat. Ut (a young Vietnamese girl) misses her mother and tries to adjust to life in the United States. Genre: realistic

Pace: compelling* **Tone:** hopeful/upbeat **Story Line:** action oriented **Characters:** vivid

15. *Apples to Oregon* by Deborah Hopkinson. Delicious helps her father and the family make a covered wagon journey from Iowa to Oregon with the family fruit trees in tow. Genre: historical

Pace: measured **Tone:** engaging **Story Line:** event oriented* (first art lesson)/character centered **Characters:** lifelike

16. *The Art Lesson* by Tomie dePaola. Tommy's first art lesson (and first art teacher) inspires him to continue pursuing his dream of being an artist. Genre: realistic

Pace: deliberate **Tone:** engaging **Story Line:** character centered **Characters:** dramatic

17. *Bartleby Speaks* by Robin Cruise. The baby Bartleby does not speak, not because he can't but because he is too busy listening. Genre: realistic

Pace: measured **Tone:** magical/timeless* **Story Line:** episodic **Characters:** recognizable

18. *Basho and the River Stones* by Tim Myers. A wily fox must make right a trick he plays on Basho by getting the poet to accept the gold coins he needs to be able to live comfortably. Genre: folktale style

Pace: unhurried **Tone:** quiet/bittersweet **Story Line:** gentle*/family centered **Characters:** recognizable

19. *Basket Moon* by Mary Lyn Ray. After being called a hillbilly by the townspeople of Hudson, a young boy is no longer certain he wants to be a basket maker like his father. Genre: historical

Pace: compelling **Tone:** magical **Story Line:** mythic* **Characters:** vivid

20. *Batwings and the Curtain of Night* by Marguerite Davol. Following the creation of day and night, the nocturnal animals must find a way to let some light through the curtain of night. Genre: creation myth

Pace: easy **Tone:** heartwarming/hopeful **Story Line:** issue oriented/thought provoking* **Characters:** realistic

21. *Beatrice's Goat* by Page McBrier. The course of a Ugandan family's life is radically altered for the better when they receive a goat as a gift. Genre: realistic

Pace: compelling **Tone:** magical* **Story Line:** mystical*/gentle **Characters:** evocative*

22. *Big Wolf and Little Wolf—The Leaf that Wouldn't Fall* by Nadine Brun-Cosme. Little Wolf is desperate to have the tiny leaf at the very top of a tree. He is certain there is much about it that is magical. When Big Wolf risks injury to get it for him, he wonders if the leaf is worth it. His initial suspicions about the leaf's otherworldly worth are confirmed in the end. Genre: allegory

Pace: leisurely **Tone:** detailed setting* **Story Line:** family centered/setting oriented **Characters:** evocative

23. *Bigmama's* by Donald Crews. Year after year, things stay the same at Bigmama's home in the country, and the family's yearly visits bring reassurance that this will always be so. Genre: autobiographical

Pace: measured **Tone:** gritty* **Story Line:** setting oriented **Characters:** recognizable

24. *Black Cat* by Christopher Myers. A black cat roams the neighborhood where it lives, exploring as it does. Genre: verse

Pace: densely written **Tone:** engaging **Story Line:** action oriented **Characters:** vivid* 25. *Black Cowboy Wild Horses: A True Story* by Julius Lester. Black cowboy Bob Lemmons single-handedly delivers a herd of wild mustangs to a corral. Genre: biography/historical
Pace: lively **Tone:** magical/heartwarming **Story Line:** complex* **Characters:** evocative 26. *Blueberry Girl* by Neil Gaiman. A parent's plea for his Blueberry Girl's life to be all that it can possibly be. Genre: verse
Pace: deliberate **Tone:** magical **Story Line:** action oriented **Characters:** familiar 27. *The Boy Who Wouldn't Obey—A Mayan Legend* by Anne Rockwell. In the end, not being obedient helps a young boy get back to the family he misses terribly. Genre: legend
Pace: fast/lively **Tone:** humorous **Story Line:** multiple plot lines* **Characters:** vivid 28. *The Boy, the Bear, the Baron, the Bard* by Gregory Rogers. A young boy inadvertently travels back in time to Shakespearean England and finds himself being chased by the bard on a madcap adventure. Genre: wordless/historical
Pace: measured **Tone:** engaging **Story Line:** inspirational **Characters:** well developed* 29. *Brave Irene* by William Steig. Irene bravely and persistently battles a snowstorm to deliver a ball gown her mother has sewn for the duchess. Genre: realistic
Pace: fast/lively **Tone:** humorous **Story Line:** character centered* **Characters:** quirky 30. *But Excuse Me That Is My Book* by Lauren Child. Lola will not accept that "her" book has been checked out of the library and will not accept substitutes suggested by her brother Charlie. Genre: realistic
Pace: unhurried **Tone:** suspenseful* **Story Line:** domestic **Characters:** recognizable 31. *Cassie's Sweet Berry Pie: A Civil War Story* by Karen Winnick. A young Southern girl fools a group of Yankee soldiers into leaving by pretending her brother and sister have the measles. Genre: historical
Pace: compelling **Tone:** bleak*/sad **Story Line:** event oriented **Characters:** evocative 32. *The Cats in Krasinski Square* by Karen Hesse. A plan to smuggle food into the Warsaw Ghetto is aided by the stray cats that roam in and out of the area. Genre: historical
Pace: easy **Tone:** quiet/sad/heavy* **Story Line:** gentle **Characters:** well developed 33. *Cherry and Olive* by Benjamin Lacombe. Cherry is lonely and painfully shy until she befriends a dog (Olive) at the shelter where her father works. Genre: realistic
Pace: lively* **Tone:** humorous **Story Line:** action oriented **Characters:** quirky 34. *The Chicken Chasing Queen of Lamar County* by Janice Harrington. A young farm girl calls herself the Chicken Chasing Queen and is determined to catch her favorite hen until she learns something about the hen that makes her change her mind about capturing the bird. Genre: realistic
Pace: easy **Tone:** humorous **Story Line:** issue oriented* **Characters:** well developed 35. *Chrysanthemum* by Kevin Henkes. Chrysanthemum loves her name until she starts school and her classmates make fun of it. Genre: realistic (if you think of the animals as humans)
Pace: fast **Tone:** humorous **Story Line:** action oriented **Characters:** quirky* 36. *Click, Clack, Moo: Cows That Type* by Doreen Cronin. Farmer Brown's cows find an old typewriter in the barn and begin to type demands and go on strike when these are not met. Genre: fantasy
Pace: fast **Tone:** n/a **Story Line:** fact filled* **Characters:** n/a 37. *Cloud Dance* by Thomas Locker. A variety of clouds dance across the sky at various times of day. Includes facts about each of the different types of clouds. Genre: natural science
Pace: engrossing **Tone:** magical* **Story Line:** resolved ending **Characters:** dramatic 38. *Cloudy With a Chance of Meatballs* by Judi Barett. In the town of Chewandswallow, food rains from the sky three times a day, until unpredictable weather forces the citizens to find another place to live. Genre: tall tale/magical realism

Pace: unhurried **Tone:** quiet **Story Line:** domestic/family centered **Characters:** evocative*

    39. *Coming on Home Soon* by Jacqueline Woodson. Ada Ruth's mother leaves her with her grandmother and goes off to find work on the railroads. Ada Ruth longs for word from her mother and her eventual return. Genre: historical/realistic

Pace: deliberate **Tone:** foreboding/magical* **Story Line:** open ended* **Characters:** dramatic

    40. *The Crane Wife* by Odds Bodkin. A retold folktale about a poor sail maker married to a mysterious bride who has the ability to weave magical sails. Genre: folktale (retold)

Pace: stately* **Tone:** mystical **Story Line:** character centered **Characters:** well developed

    41. *Crazy Horse's Vision* by Joseph Bruchac. A story of the early life of Crazy Horse, defender of the Lakota people. Genre: legend

Pace: measured **Tone:** spooky* **Story Line:** layered **Characters:** dramatic

    42. *The Crow (A Not So Scary Story)* by Alison Paul. A small boy fears the creature outside his window and imagines it to be a number of threatening things before realizing it is a crow. Genre: verse

Pace: measured **Tone:** dark/sad* **Story Line:** thought provoking **Characters:** familiar

    43. *The Crystal Heart* by Aaron Shepard. A beautiful young Vietnamese princess comes to regret her cruelty toward a humble fisherman. Genre: legend

Pace: easy **Tone:** heartwarming/hopeful/magical **Story Line:** gentle **Characters:** quirky

    44. *The Curious Garden* by Peter Brown. A magical garden (tended by a young boy) explores the city and thereby grows to cover more and more of it. Genre: magical realism

Pace: deliberate **Tone:** bittersweet/heavy* **Story Line:** domestic/family centered **Characters:** evocative

    45. *Dandelions* by Eve Bunting. Zoe and her family venture west to the Nebraska Territory. Relying on each other for support, the family faces the loneliness and desolation of frontier living. Genre: historical

Pace: deliberate **Tone:** humorous **Story Line:** action oriented **Characters:** recognizable

    46. *The Day I Swapped My Dad for Two Goldfish* by Neil Gaiman. A young boy trades his father for two goldfish. Then he and his sister go on a quest to get him back. Genre: realistic/humorous

Pace: deliberate **Tone:** detailed setting*/suspenseful **Story Line:** layered* **Characters:** lifelike

    47. *The Day of Ahmed's Secret* by Florence Parry and Judith Heide Gilliland. Throughout his workday delivering fuel in Cairo, Ahmed looks forward to sharing his secret with his family. Genre: realistic

Pace: relaxed **Tone:** heartwarming **Story Line:** gentle/family centered **Characters:** vivid*

    48. *Dear Juno* by Soyung Pak. Juno finds a way to communicate with his grandmother in Korea without having to write or read. Genre: realistic

Pace: fast **Tone:** engaging/humorous **Story Line:** gentle* **Characters:** quirky

    49. *Dear Mr. Blueberry* by Simon James. A young girl corresponds with her teacher, trying to convince him that a blue whale lives in her family's pond. Genre: realistic

Pace: fast **Tone:** humorous **Story Line:** episodic **Characters:** vivid

    50. *Dear Vampa* by Ross Collins. When the Wolfsons move next door, a young vampire writes to his grandfather recounting all the ways in which the family cannot adjust to their odd and different behaviors. Genre: allegory

Pace: leisurely **Tone:** bittersweet* **Story Line:** issue oriented/open ended **Characters:** introspective

    51. *Dear Willie Rudd* by Libba Moore Gray. An adult woman remembers her childhood and her relationship with a Black woman and wishes she could apologize to her for any wrong that was done to her due to race. Genre: realistic

Pace: easy **Tone:** suspenseful **Story Line:** plot centered* **Characters:** vivid

    52. *Doctor De Soto* by William Steig. Dr. DeSoto (a mouse and a dentist) and his wife outsmart a fox with plans to eat them. Genre: animal story

Pace: relaxed **Tone:** heartwarming* **Story Line:** resolved ending **Characters:** recognizable

53. *The Dog Who Belonged to No One* by Amy Hest. In the midst of a terrible storm, Lia and the dog who belonged to no one find each other and become steadfast, life-long friends. Genre: realistic

Pace: deliberate **Tone:** suspenseful/heartwarming* **Story Line:** resolved ending **Characters:** n/a

54. *Dolphins on the Sand* by Jim Arnosky. When a group of dolphins is beached on a sand bar, humans intervene and help them return to deeper waters. Includes factual notes about the phenomenon of beached dolphins. Genre: natural science

Pace: easy **Tone:** magical* **Story Line:** fact filled **Characters:** n/a

55. *Dream Weaver* by Jonathan London. A young boy sees the world through a spider's-eye view. Genre: natural science/spiders

Pace: lively **Tone:** humorous **Story Line:** action oriented/resolved ending **Characters:** quirky/recognizable

56. *The Dunderheads* by Paul Fleischman. The Dunderheads prove to their mean teacher that they are not stupid at all. Genre: realistic/humorous

Pace: lively **Tone:** melodramatic **Story Line:** mythic* **Characters:** vivid

57. *Dust Devil* by Anne Isaacs. Swamp Angel and Dust Devil's epic battle with Backward Bart and his Flying Desperadoes gives rise to the Grand Canyon, Montana's buttes and geysers, and the Sawtooth Range. Genre: tall tale

Pace: fast **Tone:** humorous **Story Line:** family centered **Characters:** recognizable/well drawn*

58. *Earrings!* by Judith Viorst. A young girl wants only one thing: earrings for pierced ears. Her parents want her to wait. She wants them NOW. Genre: realistic

Pace: leisurely **Tone:** magical* **Story Line:** character centered **Characters:** quirky

59. *Earth to Audrey* by Susan Hughes. Far from being from another planet, Audrey is very much in touch with Earth and all its wonders. Genre: realistic

Pace: measured **Tone:** humorous **Story Line:** character centered* **Characters:** recognizable

60. *Edwardo: The Horriblest Boy in the Whole Wide World* by John Burningham. Edwardo starts out being an ordinary boy who misbehaves occasionally but whose misbehaviors are blown out of proportion by the adults in his life until he actually does become the horrible boy they say he is. A change in the adults' perceptions of Edwardo's behavior leads to an actual change in the boy. Genre: realistic

Pace: stately* **Tone:** magical **Story Line:** inspirational **Characters:** eccentric/introspective

61. *Emily* by Michael Bedard. An exchange of special gifts with a little girl brings friendship into the life of the reclusive Emily. Genre: biography (Emily Dickinson)

Pace: compelling **Tone:** timeless* **Story Line:** character centered **Characters:** familiar

62. *The Emperor and the Kite* by Jane Yolen. The emperor's smallest daughter is completely ignored and unloved until she is the only one of his children capable of coming up with a plan to rescue him from his imprisonment. Genre: folktale (retold)

Pace: stately **Tone:** dark/foreboding/menacing* **Story Line:** issue oriented **Characters:** dramatic

63. *Encounter* by Jane Yolen. Columbus' discovery of America told from the viewpoint of a young Taino Indian boy whose dreams presage the natives' downfall. Genre: historical

Pace: relaxed **Tone:** heartwarming **Story Line:** resolved ending **Characters:** recognizable

64. *Farfallina & Marcel* by Holly Keller. Farfallina the caterpillar and Marcel the goose are great friends, separated temporarily as each of them grows. Includes factual notes on butterflies. Genre: animal story

Pace: measured **Tone:** edgy/dark **Story Line:** issue oriented/thought provoking* **Characters:** recognizable

65. *Feathers and Fools* by Mem Fox. In fear of each other's differences, a group of swans and a group of peacocks end up exterminating each other. Think: arms race. Genre: allegory/fable

Pace: lively **Tone:** menacing **Story Line:** resolved ending **Characters:** recognizable

66. *Fergus and the Night Demon: An Irish Ghost Story* by Jim Murphy. Fergus changes his lazy ways following an encounter with the Night Demon. Genre: ghost story

Pace: engrossing **Tone:** magical* **Story Line:** mystical **Characters:** quirky

67. *Fiona's Luck* by Teresa Bateman. Fiona outwits the king of the leprechauns and gets luck back for the people of Ireland. Genre: folktale

Pace: engrossing **Tone:** bittersweet/magical* **Story Line:** gentle **Characters:** evocative

68. *Fireflies!* by Julie Brinckloe. A young boy takes great pleasure in having caught hundreds of fireflies but soon afterward realizes that if he does not release them, they will die. Genre: realistic

Pace: measured **Tone:** bleak/sad* **Story Line:** issue oriented **Characters:** realistic/evocative*

69. *Fly Away Home* by Eve Bunting. A young boy and his father are homeless and live in an airport, trying not to get caught by security agents. Genre: realistic

Pace: unhurried **Tone:** suspenseful **Story Line:** resolved ending* **Characters:** well developed

70. *Fly High Fly Low* by Don Freeman. A pigeon's decision to make his home in a letter that is part of a large sign turns out to have been a great idea—but only after a frightening episode is done. Genre: animal story

Pace: relaxed **Tone:** humorous **Story Line:** character centered **Characters:** quirky

71. *The Fortune Tellers* by Lloyd Alexander. Tired of life as a carpenter, a young man pays a visit to a fortuneteller whose predictions come true in surprising ways. Genre: folktale

Pace: measured **Tone:** bittersweet/sad/quiet **Story Line:** gentle/thought provoking* **Characters:** evocative/lifelike

72. *Four Feet, Two Sandals* by Karen Lynne Williams and Khadra Mohammed. Two young girls living in a refugee camp share one pair of sandals between them until the day one of the girls learns her family will be leaving the camp for America. Genre: realistic/problem

Pace: lively **Tone:** humorous **Story Line:** gentle* **Characters:** familiar

73. *Fred Stays With Me* by Nancy Coffelt. A young child describes how sometimes she lives with her mother and sometimes she lives with her father. Her dog Fred, however, is always with her—regardless of where she is. Genre: realistic

Pace: measured **Tone:** magical/engaging **Story Line:** inspirational*/character centered **Characters:** quirky

74. *Frederick* by Leo Lionni. Frederick's poetry helps the rest of the field mice make it through a long, cold winter. Genre: animal story

Pace: lively **Tone:** magical* **Story Line:** resolved ending **Characters:** quirky

75. *The Funny Little Woman* by Arlene Mosel. The funny little woman escapes from the wicked Oni with a magic paddle that enables her to make large numbers of dumplings easily. Genre: folktale (retold)

Pace: lively **Tone:** engaging **Story Line:** plot twist* **Characters:** familiar

76. *Gator Gumbo* by Candace Fleming. In a twist on the tale of the Little Red Hen, an old alligator comes up with a way to trick the three animals that tease him into becoming the special ingredients in his gumbo. Genre: animal story/trickster tale

Pace: lively **Tone:** humorous **Story Line:** character centered/episodic* **Characters:** series characters

77. *George and Martha* by James Marshall. Five stories about two hippos (George and Martha) and their friendship. Genre: short stories

Pace: unhurried **Tone:** quiet/timeless* **Story Line:** character centered/inspirational characters: introspective

78. *Georgia Rises: A Day in the Life of Georgia O'Keefe* by Kathryn Lasky. A glimpse into the daily painting life of artist Georgia O'Keeffe. Set in New Mexico. Includes biographical notes at the end. Genre: biography (Georgia O'Keefe)

Pace: measured **Tone:** engaging **Story Line:** family centered **Characters:** vivid
79. *The Giant Carrot* by Jan Peck. Papa, Mama, and Brother Abel are growing a carrot, but it is Sweet Little Isabel's singing and dancing that make the carrot grow the most. Genre: folktale (adapted)

Pace: unhurried **Tone:** magical/sad **Story Line:** gentle **Characters:** evocative
80. *The Girl in the Castle Inside the Museum* by Kate Bernheimer. A little girl lives a life of loneliness inside a castle inside a museum. The only time her loneliness eases is when children visit the museum. Genre: Fantasy

Pace: engaging **Tone:** foreboding at first, then bittersweet **Story Line:** inspirational* **Characters:** lifelike
81. *Goal!* by Mina Javaherbin. In a township in South Africa, a group of soccer-playing boys band together against a threatening group of bullies. Genre: realistic

Pace: compelling **Tone:** bittersweet **Story Line:** issue oriented* **Characters:** vivid
82. *Goin' Someplace Special* by Patricia McKissack. Tricia Ann confronts segregation and Jim Crow laws on a journey to the desegregated public library and finds strength and pride in her grandmother's words. Genre: historical

Pace: easy **Tone:** bittersweet **Story Line:** family centered/issue oriented **Characters:** introspective
83. *Going Home* by Eve Bunting. A young Mexican boy comes to learn of the sacrifices his mother and father have made to give him and his sisters opportunities in the United States. Genre: realistic

Pace: measured **Tone:** bittersweet **Story Line:** issue oriented*/fact filled **Characters:** realistic
84. *Going North* by Janice Harrington. In the summer of 1964, a family of African Americans leaves Alabama and drives to Nebraska to escape racism and segregation and make a new life for themselves. Genre: historical/realistic

Pace: compelling **Tone:** dark/foreboding* **Story Line:** mystical **Characters:** dramatic
85. *Golem* by David Wisniewski. In sixteenth-century Prague, a rabbi creates a clay creature (golem) to protect the Jews from persecution. Genre: historical/magical realism

Pace: easy **Tone:** engaging **Story Line:** action oriented* **Characters:** vivid
86. *Good Enough to Eat* by Brock Cole. A poor young girl is sacrificed by her town to an ogre but ends up outwitting all the townspeople and earning her keep in the process. Genre: fairy tale

Pace: measured **Tone:** bittersweet* **Story Line:** episodic **Characters:** recognizable
87. *The Good Luck Cat* by Joy Harjo. Woogie, the lucky cat, uses up her nine lives one by one. Her luck, however, does not run out. Genre: realistic

Pace: fast **Tone:** foreboding then heartwarming **Story Line:** issue oriented* (judging) **Characters:** familiar
88. *Gorilla! Gorilla!* by Jeanne Willis. A mother mouse is in search of her lost baby and in fear of the gorilla that is following her wherever she goes. Genre: animal story

Pace: deliberate **Tone:** suspenseful **Story Line:** action oriented* **Characters:** quirky
89. *Gorky Rises* by William Steig. Gorky the frog creates a magic potion that enables him to fly. Genre: magical realism

Pace: unhurried **Tone:** bittersweet **Story Line:** family centered **Characters:** introspective*
90. *Grandfather's Journey* by Allen Say. A Japanese American man retells the story of his grandfather's migration from Japan to California (and back) and explores his own deep conflict over where home really is. Genre: historical/realistic

Pace: unhurried **Tone:** bittersweet **Story Line:** issue oriented*/fact filled **Characters:** realistic
91. *Grandmama's Pride* by Becky Birtha. In the summer of 1956, six-year-old Sarah Marie travels to the South to visit her grandmother and experiences segregation. On a return visit the following summer, Sarah Marie discovers a number of changes. Genre: historical/realistic

Pace: fast **Tone:** heartwarming* **Story Line:** issue oriented **Characters:** recognizable
92. *Grandmother's Garden* by John Archambault. In Grandmother Rose's garden, children of all races and from all over the world are one. Genre: verse

Pace: unhurried **Tone:** humorous **Story Line:** action oriented **Characters:** quirky*
93. *Grandpa's Teeth* by Rod Clement. Grandpa's teeth are missing. No one is above suspicion, and the entire town is being investigated. Genre: mystery/realistic

Pace: easy **Tone:** quiet **Story Line:** setting oriented*/gentle **Characters:** n/a
94. *The Great Blue House* by Kate Banks. Describes a year of seasons in a summer home—especially the activity in the house when the family is not there. Genre: realistic

Pace: relaxed **Tone:** quiet/timeless* **Story Line:** gentle **Characters:** recognizable
95. *Great Joy* by Kate DiCamillo. Frances invites a homeless organ grinder and his monkey to attend her church Christmas pageant. Genre: realistic

Pace: unhurried **Tone:** engaging **Story Line:** issue oriented*/fact filled **Characters:** n/a
96. *The Great Kapok Tree: A Tale of the Amazon Rain Forest* by Lynne Cherry. One by one, the animal inhabitants of a kapok tree convince a man not to chop down their beloved home. To persuade the man, each animal points out a consequence of the tree's removal from the rain forest. Genre: natural science

Pace: engrossing **Tone:** humorous **Story Line:** character centered* **Characters:** vivid*
97. *Greedy Zebra* by Mwenye Hadithi. A tale of how animals got their furs, skins, and horns and how zebras ended up with a black-and-white-striped coat. Genre: folktale

Pace: lively **Tone:** humorous/magical **Story Line:** resolved ending **Characters:** recognizable
98. *The Hair of Zoe Fleefenbacher Goes to School* by Laurie Halse Anderson. Zoe's hair is wild and capable of action on its own. This suits everyone just fine until Zoe reaches first grade and encounters a teacher who has rules for everything—including Zoe's hair. Genre: magical realism/humorous

Pace: unhurried **Tone:** hopeful*/suspenseful **Story Line:** family centered/issue oriented **Characters:** lifelike
99. *Hannah Is My Name* by Belle Yang. Hannah and her family eagerly await the arrival of the green cards that will make them citizens of the United States. Genre: realistic

Pace: deliberate **Tone:** dark/heavy*/grimly hopeful in the end **Story Line:** inspirational **Characters:** introspective
100. *The Harmonica* by Tony Johnston. During WWII, a young Polish boy is separated from his parents and sent to a concentration camp, where he plays the harmonica for a commandant and finds hope in music. Genre: historical

Pace: stately* **Tone:** timeless **Story Line:** domestic/family centered **Characters:** detailed
101. *Hattie and the Waves* by Barbara Cooney. In her own time and way, Hattie finally determines to become a painter. Genre: historical

Pace: fast **Tone:** humorous **Story Line:** character centered **Characters:** recognizable
102. *Hattie the Bad* by Jane Devlin. Hattie starts out being very bad, goes on to be very good, then finally finds a happy medium between the two. Genre: realistic

Pace: measured **Tone:** engaging/heartwarming **Story Line:** family centered* **Characters:** recognizable
103. *The Have a Good Day Café* by Frances and Ginger Park. A Korean family's food cart business is doing poorly until the grandmother (newly arrived from Korea) takes matters into her own hands and helps the family business thrive. Genre: realistic

Pace: measured **Tone:** bittersweet **Story Line:** complex/layered* **Characters:** quirky
104. *The Heart and the Bottle* by Oliver Jeffers. A perennially curious girl loses her "heart" and with it her curiosity—until an equally curious child leads her back to it. Genre: allegory

Pace: leisurely **Tone:** engaging/heartwarming/upbeat* **Story Line:** family centered **Characters:** quirky

105. *The Hello, Goodbye Window* by Norton Juster. A window in her grandparents' home gives a little girl a special view of time spent with her Nanna and Poppy. Genre: realistic

Pace: measured **Tone:** melodramatic **Story Line:** issue oriented **Characters:** lifelike

106. *Hen Hears Gossip* by Megan McDonald. Hen overhears "news" on the farm. As it makes its way through the rest of the animals, it changes into something completely different. Genre: realistic (if you think of the animals as humans)

Pace: relaxed **Tone:** magical **Story Line:** mythic/plot twists* **Characters:** vivid

107. *Hewitt Anderson's Great Big Life* by Jerdine Nolen. Despite being quite small (compared to his gigantic parents), Hewitt Anderson lives "large," and in several surprising twists, repeatedly rescues his parents. Genre: tall tale

Pace: deliberate **Tone:** nightmare* **Story Line:** tragic/event oriented **Characters:** n/a (it's about the event)

108. *Hiroshima No Pika* by Toshi Maruki. A retelling of the dropping of the atomic bomb on Hiroshima and the impact on a little girl and her family. Genre: historical

Pace: deliberate **Tone:** humorous **Story Line:** character centered* **Characters:** detailed

109. *Hogwood Steps Out: A Good, Good Pig Story* by Howard Mansfield. Hogwood the pig thoroughly enjoys escaping his pen and causing havoc for gardeners. Genre: animal story

Pace: unhurried **Tone:** quiet **Story Line:** gentle **Characters:** recognizable

110. *Hondo and Fabian* by Peter McCarty. A day in the lives of a dog (Hondo) and a cat (Fabian). Hondo visits the beach, while Fabian stays home with the baby. Genre: realistic

Pace: deliberate **Tone:** timeless **Story Line:** issue oriented **Characters:** recognizable

111. *The Honest-to-Goodness Truth* by Patricia McKissack. Libby learns the difference between truth telling that is good and truth telling that is unnecessarily hurtful. Genre: realistic

Pace: compelling **Tone:** suspenseful **Story Line:** family centered*/issue oriented **Characters:** realistic

112. *How Many Days to America? A Thanksgiving Story* by Eve Bunting. A family undertakes a dangerous boat journey from the Caribbean to America, arriving on Thanksgiving Day and finding much to be grateful for. Genre: realistic

Pace: deliberate **Tone:** engaging **Story Line:** character centered **Characters:** recognizable*

113. *I Hate English* by Ellen Levine. Mei Mei refuses to speak English and wishes she were living back in Hong Kong and not in New York City. Genre: realistic

Pace: fast **Tone:** humorous* **Story Line:** setting oriented **Characters:** realistic

114. *I Hate School* by Jeanne Willis. Honor Brown absolutely hates school for ever so many wild reasons . . . or does she? Genre: realistic/verse

Pace: engrossing **Tone:** bittersweet **Story Line:** family centered/hopeful **Characters:** introspective*

115. *I Have an Olive Tree* by Eve Bunting. Following her grandfather's death, Sophia and her mother journey to Greece, where she learns about her family's roots. Genre: realistic

Pace: lively **Tone:** humorous **Story Line:** character centered* **Characters:** familiar

116. *I Will Never Not Ever Eat a Tomato* by Lauren Child. Charlie convinces his picky sister Lola to eat all the foods she says she will never eat by claiming they are something else completely. Genre: realistic

Pace: relaxed **Tone:** timeless **Story Line:** domestic/family centered* **Characters:** evocative

117. *I, Doko—The Tale of a Basket* by Ed Young. A Nepalese basket recounts the many ways in which it has been used over the years by three generations of one family. Genre: fable (retold)

Pace: lively **Tone:** humorous* **Story Line:** action oriented **Characters:** familiar

118. *Iggy Peck, Architect* by Andrea Beaty. Iggy Peck wants nothing more in life than to build structures and one day become an architect. His teacher comes around to seeing things his way when his skills rescue the class on a school trip gone bad. Genre: verse/realistic

Pace: relaxed **Tone:** magical* **Story Line:** gentle **Characters:** evocative
119. *Immi's Gift* by Karin Littlewood. Immi uses the brightly colored objects she fishes out of the icy water to decorate her igloo and bring color to her winter. In spring, before leaving, she drops a gift of her own into the water. Genre: magical realism

Pace: unhurried **Tone:** magical* **Story Line:** family centered **Characters:** recognizable
120. *In a Blue Room* by Jim Averbeck. Alice will not go to sleep until everything in her room is blue. Her mother does all she can to get Alice to sleep. Genre: realistic

Pace: lively **Tone:** engaging **Story Line:** resolved ending * **Characters:** vivid
121. *Inch by Inch* by Leo Lionni. An inchworm measures various birds' body parts to avoid being eaten. When he is asked to measure a nightingale's song, he tricks the bird and manages to escape. Genre: animal story

Pace: deliberate* **Tone:** humorous **Story Line:** family centered/gentle **Characters:** recognizable
122. *Ira Sleeps Over* by Bernard Waber. Ira struggles with the idea of bringing his teddy bear to a sleep over at his friend's house. Genre: realistic

Pace: fast **Tone:** melodramatic* **Story Line:** action oriented **Characters:** dramatic
123. *The Island of the Skog* by Steven Kellog. A band of mice escapes to a faraway island and ultimately befriends its one inhabitant (a skog), but not before their aggressive initial behavior is seen as having been unnecessary. Genre: fantasy

Pace: measured **Tone:** humorous **Story Line:** domestic*/resolved ending **Characters:** familiar
124. *It Could Always Be Worse* by Margot Zemach. A poor man thinks his home life couldn't possibly be worse until the rabbi suggests he bring his animals into his house to live with his large family. Genre: folktale (retold)

Pace: engrossing **Tone:** magical **Story Line:** resolved ending **Characters:** quirky
125. *Jennie's Hat* by Ezra Jack Keats. When the hat Jennie receives from her aunt seems dull to her, the birds she feeds every week help to embellish it and turn it from plain to spectacular. Genre: magical realism

Pace: fast **Tone:** humorous **Story Line:** rich and famous* **Characters:** eccentric*
126. *King Bidgood's in the Bathtub* by Audrey Wood. King Bidgood refuses to get out of the tub despite the repeated attempts of his courtiers to get him to do so. Genre: fairy tale–like

Pace: lively **Tone:** hopeful **Story Line:** character centered*/resolved ending **Characters:** recognizable
127. *Kitten's First Full Moon* by Kevin Henkes. A tiny kitten mistakes the first full moon she's ever seen for a bowl of milk and ends up exhausting herself trying to reach it. Genre: realistic

Pace: lively **Tone:** heartwarming* **Story Line:** family centered **Characters:** lifelike
128. *Koala Lou* by Mem Fox. Koala Lou hatches a plan to get her extremely busy mother's attention and ends up discovering her mother never stopped loving her even if she did get too busy to tell her so. Genre: realistic (f you think of the animals as humans)

Pace: lively **Tone:** engaging/hopeful **Story Line:** character centered* **Characters:** quirky
129. *Leo the Late Bloomer* by Robert Kraus. In this allegory for delayed development, Leo blooms in his own time. Genre: allegory

Pace: compelling **Tone:** quiet/sad* **Story Line:** event oriented **Characters:** introspective
130. *Letting Go Swift River* by Jane Yolen. Many years after the flooding of Swift River Valley, a young woman is finally able to let go of the memory of the town of her childhood. Includes factual details about the actual event at the beginning of the book. Genre: realistic

Pace: relaxed **Tone:** engaging **Story Line:** fact filled **Characters:** well developed*
131. *The Librarian Who Measured the Earth* by Kathryn Lasky. Describes the life and work of Eratosthenes (the Greek scholar/librarian), who accurately measured the circumference of the earth more than 2,000 years ago. Genre: biography

Pace: leisurely **Tone:** magical/upbeat **Story Line:** character centered **Characters:** detailed/well developed*

132. *Lily Brown's Paintings* by Angela Johnson. Lily Brown's paintings are complete expressions of her playful imagination. Genre: realistic

---

Pace: compelling **Tone:** mystical*/suspenseful **Story Line:** action oriented **Characters:** well drawn

133. *Little Eagle* by Chen Jiang Hong. Master Yang rescues and trains Little Eagle in the secrets of eagle boxing martial arts. Genre: folktale-like

---

Pace: fast **Tone:** bittersweet **Story Line:** issue oriented/resolved ending* **Characters:** lifelike

134. *The Little Matador* by Julian Hector. The Little Matador would rather draw animals than fight bulls. At first his parents are disappointed, but eventually they realize he must follow his dreams. Genre: realistic

---

Pace: unhurried **Tone:** bittersweet/quiet* **Story Line:** gentle **Characters:** n/a

135. *The Little Yellow Leaf* by Carin Berger. A little yellow leaf hangs on to his branch, refusing to drop despite the change in season—until a red leaf on the same tree gives him the courage to let go. Genre: magical realism

---

Pace: measured **Tone:** magical/quiet* **Story Line:** event oriented **Characters:** dramatic

136. *The Longest Night* by Marion Dane Bauer. The wind knows that a crow, a moose, and a fox will not succeed in bringing back the sun to warm up the long cold, dark winter night. The wind also knows that a small chickadee's song will work. Genre: verse

---

Pace: easy **Tone:** bittersweet **Story Line:** character centered* **Characters:** lifelike

137. *Looking After Louis* by Lesley Ely. A little girl looks after and helps her autistic classmate Louis. In the process, she learns to accept his differences. Includes factual notes about autism at the end. Genre: realistic/problem

---

Pace: lively **Tone:** engaging **Story Line:** event oriented **Characters:** dramatic

138. *Lord of the Animals: A Native American Creation Myth* by Fiona French. When the animals cannot decide on what traits to give the lord of the animals, clever Coyote decides for them by combining many of the traits they each suggested. Genre: mythology

---

Pace: easy **Tone:** heartwarming* **Story Line:** gentle* **Characters:** evocative

139. *Louie* by Ezra Jack Keats. Louie is quiet and introverted until two neighborhood children reach him by unselfishly parting with a puppet Louie desperately wants. Genre: realistic

---

Pace: unhurried **Tone:** engaging **Story Line:** episodic* **Characters:** dramatic

140. *Louise, the Adventures of a Chicken* by Kate DiCamillo. Following each of her adventures, Louise the chicken is relieved and happy to be back in the warm, safe hen house with her companions. Genre: animal story

---

Pace: lively* **Tone:** humorous **Story Line:** action oriented **Characters:** vivid

141. *Love and Roast Chicken* by Barbara Knutson. Cuy the guinea pig repeatedly tricks Tio Antonio the fox into not eating him for supper. Genre: trickster tale

---

Pace: lively **Tone:** humorous **Story Line:** issue oriented **Characters:** familiar

142. *The Luck of the Loch Ness Monster* by A. W. Flaherty. On a sea voyage to Scotland, Katerina Elizabeth refuses to eat the oatmeal she is served every day. Each time she throws it overboard, a small worm eats it and grows gradually into the Loch Ness monster. Genre: magical realism

---

Pace: measured **Tone:** quiet*/bittersweet **Story Line:** domestic/family centered **Characters:** lifelike

143. *Ma Dear's Aprons* by Patricia McKissack. David Earle always knows what day of the week it is based on what apron his mother wears to work as a housekeeper in the homes of others. Genre: historical

---

Pace: lively **Tone:** upbeat* **Story Line:** character centered **Characters:** realistic

144. *Madeline* by Ludwig Bemelmans. Madeline fears nothing—not even having to go to the hospital to have her appendix removed. Genre: realistic

Pace: engrossing **Tone:** timeless **Story Line:** inspirational* **Characters:** introspective
145. *The Magic Pillow* by Demi. Ping feels badly about his family's poverty until he encounters a magician who teaches him that only internal peace is of lasting value. Genre: folktale

Pace: compelling **Tone:** suspenseful **Story Line:** action oriented **Characters:** lifelike
146. *Magnus at the Fire* by Jennifer Armstrong. Magnus the fire horse earns his retirement after helping to pull the broken-down new steam engine to a fire. Includes factual notes about the early days of fire fighting in New York City. Genre: historical/animal story

Pace: deliberate **Tone:** humorous **Story Line:** character centered* **Characters:** well drawn
147. *Martha Speaks* by Susan Meddaugh. The adventures and misadventures of Martha (the family dog), who starts speaking after eating a can of alphabet soup. Genre: magical realism

Pace: lively **Tone:** humorous **Story Line:** thought provoking **Characters:** quirky
148. *Max's Words* by Kate Banks. Max decides to collect words so that he can trade some of them with his brothers for coins and stamps. His words end up being worth more since they can be used to make stories. Genre: realistic

Pace: fast **Tone:** foreboding* **Story Line:** domestic **Characters:** recognizable
149. *McFig and McFly; A Tale of Jealousy, Revenge and Death* by Henrik Drescher. McFig and McFly take up competing with each other to see who can have the best home, until the competition gets completely out of hand. Think: keeping up with the Joneses. Genre: magical realism

Pace: densely written (Seuss-like language) **Tone:** exotic/magical* **Story Line:** thought provoking **Characters:** introspective
150. *Me, All Alone, at the End of the World* by M. T. Anderson. When his quiet retreat at the end of the world is transformed into a nonstop whirlwind of "fun," a young boy who prefers to be alone escapes back into solitude. Genre: magical realism

Pace: unhurried **Tone:** bittersweet* **Story Line:** issue oriented **Characters:** realistic
151. *The Memory String* by Eve Bunting. Laura struggles with accepting her stepmother Jane until she realizes that Jane does not want to replace her Mom (who died three years earlier). Genre: realistic

Pace: fast **Tone:** humorous/engaging **Story Line:** issue oriented*/fact filled **Characters:** quirky
152. *Michael Recycle* by Ellie Bethel. Michael Recycle saves the town of Abberdoo-Rimey from terminal pollution by teaching the townspeople to recycle. Ends with tips for how to live green. Genre: verse/science

Pace: unhurried **Tone:** engaging **Story Line:** layered* **Characters:** realistic
153. *The Milkman's Boy* by Donald Hall. After some time (and the illness of the youngest child), a family-owned dairy decides to begin pasteurizing its milk. Genre: historical

Pace: easy **Tone:** bittersweet **Story Line:** resolved ending **Characters:** recognizable
154. *Milo Armadillo* by Jan Fearnley. All Tallulah wants for her birthday is a fluffy pink rabbit. She is disappointed when she gets a pink armadillo but grows to love Milo deeply. Genre: realistic

Pace: leisurely **Tone:** engaging **Story Line:** action oriented/resolved ending **Characters:** quirky*
155. *Ming Lo Moves the Mountain* by Arnold Lobel. Desperate to move the mountain next to which they live, Ming Lo and his wife repeatedly consult the wise man until a solution is hit upon. Genre: folktale

Pace: engrossing **Tone:** hopeful* **Story Line:** inspirational **Characters:** lifelike
156. *Mirette on the High Wire* by Emily Arnold McCully. Mirette learns how to walk on a high wire from the boarder (Mr. Bellini) and eventually helps him overcome his recently developed fear of the wire. Genre: realistic

Pace: fast **Tone:** hopeful **Story Line:** resolved ending **Characters:** familiar
157. *Miss Nelson is Missing* by Harry Allard and James Marshall. Miss Nelson comes up with a plan to get the children of room 207 to behave. Genre: realistic

Pace: relaxed **Tone:** quiet/heartwarming **Story Line:** inspirational* **Characters:** quirky
158. *Miss Rumphius* by Barbara Cooney. Miss Rumphius accomplishes what she set out to do as a child: travel the world, live near the sea, and, most importantly, make the world more beautiful. Genre: realistic

Pace: measured/unhurried **Tone:** engaging **Story Line:** fact filled* **Characters:** n/a
159. *Mister Seahorse* by Eric Carle. Mister Seahorse drifts in the ocean, encountering other fathers tending their eggs along the way. Genre: natural science/animal story

Pace: easy **Tone:** heartwarming/hopeful **Story Line:** inspirational **Characters:** introspective
160. *Mole Music* by David McPhail. Mole invites music into his simple, quiet life by learning how to play the violin well. His gift ends up being shared widely. Genre: realistic (if you think of the animals as humans)

Pace: compelling **Tone:** hopeful/bittersweet **Story Line:** family centered/issue oriented **Characters:** realistic
161. *Molly Bannaky* by Alice McGill. Tells the story of Molly Bannaky (grandmother of Benjamin Bannaker, the African American scientist/astronomer). Includes historical notes. Genre: biography (Benjamin Banneker)

Pace: measured **Tone:** bittersweet/heartwarming **Story Line:** gentle/family centered **Characters:** evocative
162. *Momma, Where Are You From?* by Marie Brady. Momma describes the special people in her life when she was growing up and the circumstances of segregation during that time. Genre: historical

Pace: fast/lively* **Tone:** humorous **Story Line:** action oriented **Characters:** quirky
163. *The Monkey and the Crocodile* by Paul Galdone. In this trickster tale, a monkey successfully and cleverly outsmarts a crocodile. Genre: folktale

Pace: engrossing **Tone:** hopeful **Story Line:** layered*/fact filled **Characters:** multiple points of view
164. *The Moon Over Star* by Diana Hutts Aston. Retells one family's reactions and responses to the American lunar landing in 1969. Genre: historical

Pace: lively **Tone:** bittersweet **Story Line:** gentle* **Characters:** vivid
165. *Mrs. Katz and Tush* by Patricia Polacco. A young African American boy (Larnel) befriends an elderly Jewish widow (Mrs. Katz) and brings a small kitten (Tush) into her lonely life. Genre: realistic

Pace: leisurely **Tone:** sad to start, then upbeat and heartwarming **Story Line:** family centered **Characters:** lifelike
166. *Music, Music for Everyone* by Vera B. Williams. A young girl (whose grandmother is ill and whose mother is always working) plays music with her friends to make money to help her family with expenses. Genre: realistic

Pace: leisurely **Tone:** timeless*/bittersweet **Story Line:** gentle/family centered **Characters:** lifelike
167. *My Father's Boat* by Sherry Garland. A young boy spends the day with his father on the family's fishing boat and learns about the grandfather he has never met. Genre: realistic

Pace: engrossing **Tone:** hopeful* **Story Line:** inspirational* **Characters:** introspective
168. *My Heart Glow: Alice Cogswell, Thomas Gallaudet and the Birth of American Sign Language* by Emily Arnold McCully. Tells the story of how French Sign Language founds its way to the United States via the efforts of Thomas Gallaudet, Laurent Clerc, and Alice Cogswell. Includes historical notes at the end. Genre: nonfiction

Pace: leisurely **Tone:** bittersweet **Story Line:** character centered* **Characters:** recognizable
169. *My Name is Yoon* by Helen Recorvits. A young Korean girl struggles to adjust to life in America. Genre: realistic/problem

Pace: fast **Tone:** engaging **Story Line:** family centered **Characters:** quirky*
170. *Mystery Bottle* by Kristen Balouch. A young boy receives a mysterious bottle. When he opens it, a wind transports him from his Brooklyn home to the arms of his grandfather in Tehran. Genre: fantasy

Pace: unhurried **Tone:** bittersweet/hopeful **Story Line:** multiple plot lines* **Characters:** evocative
171. *Naming Liberty* by Jane Yolen. Two alternating stories are told: that of a Jewish family emigrating to America and the construction of the Statue of Liberty. Genre: historical

Pace: easy **Tone:** bittersweet* **Story Line:** family centered/issue oriented* **Characters:** lifelike/realistic
172. *Nana Upstairs & Nana Downstairs* by Tomie dePaola. Special relationships with both his grandmother and his great-grandmother help four-year-old Tommy come to terms with each of their deaths. Genre: realistic

Pace: engrossing **Tone:** humorous **Story Line:** domestic **Characters:** n/a (everyone is sleeping)
173. *The Napping House* by Audrey Wood. With just one bite, a wakeful flea wakes up a number of slumbering creatures in the Napping House. Genre: cumulative tale

Pace: fast **Tone:** humorous **Story Line:** thought provoking **Characters:** n/a
174. *Never Take a Shark to the Dentist* by Judy Barett. A list of activities one should not engage in with a variety of animals clearly (and humorously) ill suited for each of the activities. Genre: animal story/humorous

Pace: fast **Tone:** humorous/upbeat **Story Line:** setting oriented **Characters:** quirky/eccentric*
175. *Next Stop Grand Central* by Maira Kalman. A portrait of Grand Central Station, its many workers, and the wide variety of people moving through it each day. Genre: realistic/humorous

Pace: lively **Tone:** hopeful **Story Line:** issue oriented **Story Line:** familiar
176. *Nicolas, Where Have You Been?* by Leo Lionni. Nicolas (a field mouse) learns that not all birds are bad. He then teaches this to his friends. Genre: animal story

Pace: lively **Tone:** magical* **Story Line:** mythic **Characters:** vivid
177. *The Night Eater* by Ana Juan. Each day, the night eater brings the day by eating up the night until one day, an insult causes him to stop eating the night, resulting in a world without daylight. Genre: fantasy

Pace: easy **Tone:** humorous **Story Line:** issue oriented*/fact filled **Characters:** familiar
178. *Nothing* by Jon Agee. In the vein of "The Emperor's New Clothes." A shopping craze for nothing is started by a rich, silly woman. Think: mindless consumerism. Genre: fable

Pace: measured **Tone:** humorous **Story Line:** character centered **Characters:** familiar
179. *The Odious Ogre* by Norton Juster. When an ogre encounters a young girl who treats him with kindness, he is so confused by her lack of fear that he dies. Genre: fairy tale-like

Pace: engrossing **Tone:** humorous **Story Line:** character centered **Characters:** recognizable
180. *Old Cricket* by Lisa Wheeler. Old Cricket learns a lesson when he is too clever for his own good. Genre: cumulative tale

Pace: easy **Tone:** bittersweet **Story Line:** character centered **Characters:** eccentric*/well drawn
181. *Old Henry* by Joan W. Blos. Old Henry's unusual ways confound his neighbors. They insist that he change. He refuses to do so and leaves. Surprisingly, once he is gone, the neighbors miss him, and Henry misses them. Genre: verse/realistic

Pace: densely written* **Tone:** mystical/timeless **Story Line:** mystical* **Characters:** introspective
182. *Old Turtle and the Broken Truth* by Douglas Wood. A broken half-truth causes misunderstandings and hatred until a little girl (with the help of Old Turtle) finds its missing half and makes it (and humankind) whole again. Genre: allegory

Pace: unhurried **Tone:** mystical* **Story Line:** fact filled **Characters:** n/a
183. *On the Day You Were Born* by Debra Frasier. The birth of a child is celebrated by the earth. Genre: verse/natural science

Pace: engrossing **Tone:** bittersweet/hopeful* **Story Line:** resolved ending **Characters:** familiar
   184. *Once Upon a Time* by Niki Daly. Sarie struggles with learning to read until her Auntie Anna spends time reading with her every Sunday. Genre: realistic

Pace: unhurried **Tone:** hopeful* **Story Line:** issue oriented **Characters:** introspective
   185. *One Green Apple* by Eve Bunting. Farah is new to America and trying to figure out how to find her voice and fit in with her new schoolmates. Genre: realistic

Pace: unhurried **Tone:** heartwarming* **Story Line:** family centered **Characters:** realistic
   186. *The Orange Shoes* by Trinka Hayes Noble. Delly Porter and her family are poor, yet Delly ends up being able to teach others the value of that which does not cost anything. Genre: historical

Pace: unhurried **Tone:** bittersweet/hopeful **Story Line:** issue oriented/gentle **Characters:** evocative*
   187. *The Other Side* by Jacqueline Woodson. Two little girls (one white and one black) reach out to each other across the fence that separates their houses and (metaphorically) races. Genre: historical/realistic

Pace: engrossing **Tone:** sad/quiet/bittersweet **Story Line:** family centered **Characters:** vivid*
   188. *Our Gracie Aunt* by Jacqueline Woodson. A brother and sister are sent to live with their aunt when their mother neglects them. Genre: realistic/problem

Pace: easy **Tone:** humorous **Story Line:** character centered* **Characters:** well developed
   189. *Owen* by Kevin Henkes. Owen refuses to part with his fuzzy yellow blanket until one day his mother comes up with a solution. Genre: realistic (if you think of the animals as humans)

Pace: deliberate **Tone:** stark*/suspenseful/magical **Story Line:** event oriented **Characters:** evocative
   190. *Owl Moon* by Jane Yolen. A young girl and her father venture into the woods to go owling. Genre: realistic

Pace: deliberate **Tone:** humorous **Story Line:** character centered **Characters:** multiple points of view*
   191. *The Pain and the Great One* by Judy Blume. Sibling rivalry abounds as an eight-year-old girl (the Great One) and six-year-old boy (the Pain) each see the other as best loved by their parents. Genre: realistic

Pace: relaxed **Tone:** lush*/quiet **Story Line:** episode/layered **Characters:** multiple points of view
   192. *Painting the Wind* by Patricia and Emily MacLachlan. Painters of portraits, landscapes, and still-life paintings visit the boy's island in the summer, and as he watches each of them, he learns how to paint the wind. Genre: realistic

Pace: measured **Tone:** humorous **Story Line:** episodic* **Characters:** vivid
   193. *Pancakes for Supper* by Anne Isaacs. Toby outwits a number of animals on the way to Whisker Creek with her family. Genre: tall tale

Pace: leisurely **Tone:** heartwarming **Story Line:** inspirational/mystical **Characters:** eccentric*/well drawn
   194. *The Paper Crane* by Molly Bang. A mysterious stranger leaves a restaurant owner a magical gift that turns his business around. Genre: folktale

Pace: deliberate **Tone:** quiet **Story Line:** event oriented **Characters:** lifelike
   195. *The Paperboy* by Dav Pilkey. A paperboy delivers the morning papers to the sleeping town. Genre: realistic

Pace: deliberate **Tone:** suspenseful **Story Line:** issue oriented **Characters:** realistic
   196. *The Patchwork Path: A Quilt Map to Freedom* by Bettye Stroud. Hannah and her father escape to freedom with the help of the code sewn into her mother's quilt. Genre: historical

Pace: leisurely **Tone:** heartwarming **Story Line:** character centered **Characters:** vivid*
   197. *Pearl Barley and Charlie Parsley* by Aaron Blabey. Pearl and Charlie are completely different in very many ways—and that is precisely what makes them such great friends. Genre: realistic

Pace: lively **Tone:** engaging **Story Line:** action oriented* **Characters:** well drawn
   198. *Peggony Po: A Whale of a Tale* by Andrea Davis Pinkney. A young "wooden boy" (think Pinocchio) named Peggony Po captures Cetus the whale by outsmarting him. Genre: historical/tall tale

Pace: measured **Tone:** engaging **Story Line:** issue oriented **Characters:** introspective*
199. *Pennies in a Jar* by Dori Chaconas. A young boy finally faces his fear of horses when he comes up with the perfect gift to send his father (who is serving in WWII). Genre: historical
Pace: measured **Tone:** hopeful* **Story Line:** inspirational **Characters:** vivid
200. *Peppe the Lamplighter* by Elisa Bartone. An immigrant father struggles to accept his son Peppe's work as a street lamplighter in Little Italy. Genre: historical
Pace: deliberate **Tone:** magical* **Story Line:** resolved ending/thought provoking **Characters:** quirky
201. *Pezzettino* by Leo Lionni. Pezzettino (Little Piece) learns that rather than being a small part of anyone else, he is (though small) a whole on his own. Genre: allegory
Pace: deliberate **Tone:** heartwarming **Story Line:** family centered* **Characters:** recognizable
202. *Pictures from Our Vacation* by Rae Lynned Perkins. A young girl's summer vacation gets off to a rainy and disappointing start before turning into a family get-together full of memorable events and feelings. Genre: realistic
Pace: compelling/engrossing **Tone:** sad/heavy **Story Line:** inspirational/thought provoking* **Characters:** well drawn
203. *Pink and Say* by Patricia Polacco. Pink (an African American slave) and Say (a white boy) meet up while fighting for the Union during the American Civil War. Genre: historical
Pace: engrossing **Tone:** bittersweet **Story Line:** gentle **Characters:** vivid
204. *The Polar Express* by Chris Van Allsburg. A young boy's magical ride to the North Pole on the Polar Express reaffirms his belief in the existence of Santa Claus. Genre: magical realism
Pace: unhurried **Tone:** heavy then upbeat **Story Line:** character centered **Characters:** well drawn*
205. *The Poodle Who Barked at the Wind* by Charlotte Zolotow. When most of the family goes out, leaving a little poodle home alone with the father, she goes from barking at everything to not barking at all. Genre: realistic
Pace: easy **Tone:** magical **Story Line:** resolved ending* **Characters:** quirky
206. *Princess Hyacinth (The Surprising Tale of a Girl Who Floated)* by Florence Parry Heide. Because Princess Hyacinth floats, she cannot ever leave the castle and her life is a total bore—until Boy comes up with a solution that allows her to live happily with her unique problem. Genre: fairy tale
Pace: unhurried **Tone:** quiet **Story Line:** gentle* **Characters:** evocative
207. *Rabbit's Gift* by George Shannon. A turnip makes the rounds from one woodland animal to the next as each animal (having enough other food to eat) attempts to share it with another. Genre: folktale
Pace: easy **Tone:** bittersweet* **Story Line:** gentle/family centered **Characters:** realistic
208. *The Rag Coat* by Lauren Mills. Minna's rag coat is ridiculed by her schoolmates until she tells them the stories behind the scraps of fabric sewn into the coat. Genre: historical
Pace: unhurried **Tone:** bittersweet* **Story Line:** event oriented* **Characters:** realistic
209. *Rent Party Jazz* by William Miller. In 1930s New Orleans, Smilin' Jack (a trumpet player) helps Sonny and his mother raise rent money by throwing (and playing his instrument at) a rent party. Genre: historical
Pace: lively **Tone:** humorous **Story Line:** resolved ending **Characters:** quirky*
210. *The Retired Kid* by Jon Agee. Tired of being a kid, Brian decides to retire to the Happy Sunset Retirement Community—until he realizes he's got plenty of energy left to go on being a kid for a while longer. Gene: realistic/humorous
Pace: fast **Tone:** upbeat **Story Line:** event oriented **Characters:** recognizable*
211. *Roller Coaster* by Marla Frazee. A number of people take a roller coaster ride and react to it differently. Genre: realistic
Pace: relaxed **Tone:** upbeat **Story Line:** issue oriented* **Characters:** recognizable
212. *Rosie and the Nightmares* by Philip Waechter. Rosie the rabbit is terrified of monsters until she finds a way to confront her fears. Genre: realistic (if you think of the animals as humans)

Pace: deliberate **Tone:** bittersweet **Story Line:** inspirational* **Characters:** lifelike
213. *Ruby's Wish* by Yim Shirin Bridges. In China, at a time when few girls are taught to read and write, Ruby ends up going to university like her brothers and male cousins. Genre: historical

Pace: engrossing **Tone:** engaging **Story Line:** episodic* **Characters:** quirky
214. *The Scarecrow's Hat* by Ken Brown. A clever hen finds a resourceful way to solve Scarecrow's problem and gets a nest for herself in the bargain. Genre: animal story

Pace: densely written* (very descriptive) **Tone:** lush **Story Line:** setting oriented* **Characters:** n/a (It's completely about the setting).
215. *The Seashore Book* by Charlotte Zolotow. Even though he has never been there, a little boy is able to experience the seashore through his mother's descriptive words. Genre: realistic

Pace: relaxed/detailed setting **Tone:** heartwarming* **Story Line:** character centered **Characters:** vivid
216. *See the Ocean* by Estelle Condra. After spending many summers by the shore, Nellie (who is blind) is able to sense it before her brothers can see it as they approach it for yet another family vacation. Genre: realistic

Pace: compelling **Tone:** foreboding at first, then hopeful **Story Line:** character centered **Characters:** familiar
217. *Selvakumar Knew Better* by Virginia Kroll. Based on the true story of Selvakumar, a dog that saved a family member from drowning in the 2004 tsunami. Includes factual notes about earthquakes and tsunamis. Genre: realistic

Pace: lively **Tone:** engaging **Story Line:** thought provoking **Characters:** multiple points of view*
218. *Seven Blind Mice* by Ed Young. Six blind mice disagree about what a "strange Something" actually is, until the seventh blind mouse investigates more thoroughly. Genre: fable

Pace: easy **Tone:** humorous **Story Line:** character centered* **Characters:** well developed
219. *Sheila Rae, the Brave* by Kevin Henkes. Sheila Rae is brave and fearless until she gets lost taking a new way home from school and is rescued by her little sister. Genre: realistic (if you think of the animals as humans)

Pace: lively **Tone:** engaging **Story Line:** issue oriented* **Characters:** quirky
220. *She's Wearing a Dead Bird on Her Head* by Kathryn Lasky. Tells the fictionalized account of Minna Hall and Harriet Hemenway, who formed the Audubon society to stop the use of birds and bird feathers in hat making in the late nineteenth century. Genre: historical

Pace: easy **Tone:** hopeful*/bittersweet **Story Line:** complex*/inspirational **Characters:** evocative*
221. *Silent Music: A Story of Baghdad* by James Rumford. Ali uses the beauty of Arabic calligraphy to cope with the horrors of war in Baghdad. Genre: realistic

Pace: lively **Tone:** hopeful **Story Line:** character centered/resolved ending* **Characters:** well developed
222. *Small Florence—Piggy Pop Star!* by Claire Alexander. When her sisters lose their nerve in a singing competition, shy Small Florence sings fearlessly in front the large audience and wins the competition. Genre: realistic (if you think of the animals as humans)

Pace: deliberate **Tone:** hopeful **Story Line:** issue oriented*/fact filled **Characters:** realistic
223. *Smoky Night* by Eve Bunting. With the Los Angeles riots as a backdrop, neighbors learn to know more about each other before resorting to judgment. Genre: realistic

Pace: leisurely **Tone:** humorous **Story Line:** character centered* **Characters:** familiar
224. *Sneaky Weasel* by Hannah Shaw. When he throws a party and no one shows up, Sneaky Weasel learns how to be a better friend. Genre: realistic (if you think of the animals as humans)

Pace: unhurried **Tone:** magical quiet **Story Line:** gentle **Characters:** evocative
225. *Snow* by Cynthia Rylant. An ode to snow, its varied forms, and the joy and beauty it brings. Genre: realistic

Pace: relaxed **Tone:** quiet* **Story Line:** gentle **Characters:** evocative
226. *The Snowy Day* by Ezra Jack Keats. A young boy spends a day in the snow. Genre: realistic.

Pace: lively **Tone:** engaging **Story Line:** episodic* **Characters:** n/a
227. *Somewhere in the World Right Now* by Stacey Schuett. Describes what is happening in different places around the world at a given time. Genre: science/time zone

Pace: fast **Tone:** melodramatic* **Story Line:** character centered **Characters:** dramatic
228. *Sourpuss and Sweetie Pie* by Norton Juster. A little girl is sometimes "Sourpuss" and sometimes "Sweetie Pie"—mostly, however, she is the latter. Genre: realistic

Pace: unhurried **Tone:** bittersweet/heartwarming* **Story Line:** family centered/domestic* **Characters:** evocative
229. *Spuds* by Karen Hesse. Maybelle, Jack, and Eddie want to help their mother by gathering potatoes to feed the family but gather stones instead. Genre: realistic

Pace: lively **Tone:** humorous **Story Line:** inspirational* **Characters:** quirky
230. *Stand Tall Molly Lou Melon* by Patty Lovell. On her grandmother's advice, Molly Lou Melon stands tall and ultimately earns the respect of her new school mates. Genre: realistic

Pace: lively* **Tone:** humorous **Story Line:** action oriented **Characters:** recognizable
231. *Stellaluna* by Janell Cannon. Raised by birds, Stellaluna (a fruit bat) eventually learns she is a bat and not a bird at all. Genre: animal story

Pace: lively **Tone:** humorous **Story Line:** resolved ending **Characters:** recognizable
232. *Stone Soup* by Marcia Brown. Three soldiers trick a group of selfish and greedy peasants into sharing their food with them. Genre: folktale

Pace: compelling **Tone:** engaging **Story Line:** mythic* **Characters:** vivid
233. *Storm Boy* by Paul Owen Lewis. A young chief's son goes off to fish alone and ends up missing for one year, during which time he visits with the chiefs of another tribe. Genre: myth

Pace: relaxed **Tone:** humorous **Story Line:** character centered* **Characters:** well drawn
234. *The Story of Ferdinand* by Munro Leaf. Despite being big and strong, Ferdinand the bull has no interest in acting fierce and would much rather sit quietly and smell the flowers. Genre: realistic (if you think of the animals as humans)

Pace: engrossing **Tone:** magical/suspenseful **Story Line:** mystical* **Characters:** vivid
235. *The Stranger* by Chris Van Allsburg. Somehow the stranger's visit and ultimate departure from the Bailey farm are connected to the changes in weather between summer and fall. Genre: magical realism

Pace: leisurely **Tone:** engaging **Story Line:** resolved ending* **Characters:** recognizable
236. *Strega Nona* by Tomie dePaola. Big Anthony does not heed Strega Nona's warning not to touch the pasta pot and creates a problem for the town. Genre: folktale (retold)

Pace: lively **Tone:** melodramatic **Story Line:** mythic* **Characters:** vivid
237. *Swamp Angel* by Anne Isaacs. Swamp Angel and the colossal bear (Thundering Tarnation) battle each other, and, in the process, create the Tennessee Smoky Mountains and Montana's Shortgrass Prairie. Genre: tall tale

Pace: easy **Tone:** bittersweet* **Story Line:** issue oriented **Characters:** well drawn
238. *Sweet Clara and the Freedom Quilt* by Deborah Hopkinson. A young slave girl uses her sewing skills to create a quilt used as a map by slaves to escape to the North. Genre: historical

Pace: relaxed **Tone:** quiet/sad/bittersweet **Story Line:** inspirational* **Characters:** evocative
239. *Sweet, Sweet Memory* by Jacqueline Woodson. Now that her Grandpa is gone, Sarah struggles to remember and keep alive the things that he said to her. Genre: realistic

Pace: lively **Tone:** magical **Story Line:** inspirational **Characters:** quirky
240. *Swimmy* by Leo Lionni. Swimmy (a unique little black fish) teaches his friends to view their world differently and not be afraid. Genre: animal story

Pace: measured **Tone:** engaging* **Story Line:** family centered **Characters:** quirky
241. *Sylvester and the Magic Pebble* by William Steig. When Sylvester the donkey finds a magic pebble, trouble ensues. Genre: magical realism/animal story

Pace: lively **Tone:** romantic then creepy* **Story Line:** character centered **Characters:** quirky
242. *Tadpole's Promise* by Jeanne Willis. A tadpole and a caterpillar promise to love each other forever as long as neither of them changes. Clearly, this relationship is doomed. Genre: animal story

Pace: unhurried **Tone:** humorous **Story Line:** character centered **Characters:** vivid
243. *The Tale of Rabbit and Coyote* by Tony Johnston. Rabbit continues to trick Coyote time after time. Genre: folktale

Pace: measured **Tone:** exotic/magical* **Story Line:** action oriented*/resolved ending **Characters:** familiar
244. *The Tale of the Firebird* by Gennady Spirin. Prince Ivan-Tsarevich is challenged to complete a number of tasks in order to be able to satisfy his father's wish to own the magical firebird. Genre: folktale

Pace: measured **Tone:** heartwarming/magical* **Story Line:** gentle **Characters:** recognizable
245. *The Tale of the Mandarin Ducks* by Katherine Paterson. Two mandarin ducks rescue the man and woman who saved them from a life of captivity and misery. Genre: folktale

Pace: deliberate **Tone:** bittersweet **Story Line:** resolved ending* **Characters:** lifelike
246. *Tea With Milk* by Allen Say. May cannot adjust to living in Japan after having been raised in San Francisco—until she learns that "home" is not a place. Genre: realistic

Pace: unhurried **Tone:** sad* **Story Line:** gentle/family centered **Characters:** realistic
247. *The Tenth Good Thing About Barney* by Judith Viorst. A young boy deals with the death of his pet cat Barney and thinks up ten good things about the cat he misses so much. Genre: realistic

Pace: deliberate **Tone:** dark/foreboding/menacing/nightmare* **Story Line:** thought provoking **Characters:** recognizable
248. *Terrible Things: An Allegory of the Holocaust* by Eve Bunting. One by one, the different animals of the forest allow other animals to be taken away by the Terrible Things until there is no one left. Genre: allegorical tale

Pace: measured **Tone:** bittersweet/hopeful* **Story Line:** resolved ending **Characters:** familiar
249. *Thank You, Mr. Falker* by Patricia Polacco. Trisha struggles for years with learning how to read until Mr. Falker helps her achieve the goal. Genre: realistic

Pace: lively **Tone:** humorous **Story Line:** family centered* **Characters:** realistic
250. *Thanks a LOT Emily Post!* by Jennifer LaRue Huget. Four siblings are required by their mother to follow Emily Post's rules of etiquette until they turn the tables on her by making her do the same. Genre: realistic/humorous

Pace: relaxed **Tone:** heartwarming/timeless **Story Line:** family centered **Characters:** multiple points of view
251. *That's Papa's Way* by Kate Banks. A little girl tells of her day fishing with her father, the way he does things, and the way she does them. Genre: realistic

Pace: engrossing **Tone:** foreboding **Story Line:** mythic* **Characters:** distant*
252. *The Day the Stones Walked: A Tale of Easter Island* by T. A. Barron. The old stories say that the moai (the stone statues of Easter Island) come alive to protect the people in times of grave danger. Pico does not believe these stories until the day a tsunami strikes the island and he nearly drowns. Includes information about Easter Island, tsunamis, and deforestation. Genre: folktale like

Pace: lively **Tone:** exotic/upbeat **Story Line:** character centered/resolved ending **Characters:** dramatic

253. *The Duchess of Whimsy: An Absolutely Delicious Fairy Tale* by Randall de Seve. The Duchess of Whimsy and the Earl of Norm are very different from each other. When a crisis throws them together, they realize they have more in common than they thought at first. Genre: fairy tale

Pace: stately* **Tone:** quiet **Story Line:** issue oriented/multiple plot lines **Characters:** recognizable

254. *They Came From the Bronx* by Neil Waldman. In 1907, a Comanche grandmother and her grandson await the arrival of fifteen bison from the Bronx Zoo—part of a conservation effort to reintroduce the bison to the American West. Genre: historical

Pace: deliberate **Tone:** bittersweet **Story Line:** gentle **Characters:** realistic

255. *Those Shoes* by Maribeth Boelts. Unable to afford the sneakers he really wants in a size that fits him, Jeremy learns an important lesson about kindness. Genre: realistic

Pace: engrossing **Tone:** magical **Story Line:** action oriented **Characters:** familiar

256. *The Three Princes: A Tale from the Middle East* by Eric A. Kimmel. Three princes compete for the hand of a princess. Only the one who sacrifices the most will end up marrying her. Genre: folktale (retold)

Pace: unhurried **Tone:** quiet **Story Line:** gentle/family centered **Characters:** multiple points of view

257. *Through Grandpa's Eyes* by Patricia MacLachlan. Despite being blind, John's Grandpa teaches him how to "see" the way he does. Genre: realistic

Pace: easy **Tone:** sad/hopeful* **Story Line:** gentle/family centered **Characters:** realistic

258. *Tight Times* by Barbara Shook Hazen. A father and mother struggle to explain to their son why he cannot have a dog. Genre: realistic/problem

Pace: lively **Tone:** contemporary **Story Line:** issue oriented **Characters:** quirky

259. *Tin Lizzie* by Allan Drummond. Grandpa loves cars and working on them but also understands that it will be up to his grandchildren to figure out how to address the issues of pollution, oil dependence, and too much traffic. Includes notes about Henry Ford, the Tin Lizzie, and environmental issues. Genre: realistic/problem

Pace: unhurried **Tone:** bittersweet **Story Line:** gentle* **Characters:** realistic

260. *Tomas and the Library Lady* by Pat Mora. Tomas escapes the difficulties of migrant farm work by visiting the library and befriending the library lady there. Genre: realistic

Pace: measured **Tone:** humorous **Story Line:** resolved ending* **Characters:** recognizable

261. *Too Close Friends* by Roddie Shen. Two friends (pig and hippo) learn that privacy is important to maintain friendship. Genre: realistic (if you think of the animals as humans)

Pace: easy **Tone:** heartwarming **Story Line:** family centered* **Characters:** realistic

262. *Too Many Tamales* by Gary Soto. While helping her mother make tamales, Maria tries on her ring and ends up thinking she lost it in one of the 24 tamales they made together. Genre: realistic

Pace: leisurely **Tone:** heartwarming **Story Line:** character centered/resolved ending* **Characters:** multiple points of view*

263. *Toot and Puddle: Let it Snow* by Holly Hobbie. Best friends Toot and Puddle work hard to figure out what the perfect Christmas gifts would be to exchange. Genre: realistic (if you think of the animals as humans)

Pace: lively **Tone:** humorous **Story Line:** character centered* **Characters:** vivid*

264. *Tops & Bottoms* by Janet Stevens. Resourceful Hare tricks lazy Bear into giving him the best parts of three different crops until Bear realizes the problem is not Hare but his own laziness. Genre: folktale

Pace: measured* **Tone:** engaging **Story Line:** n/a **Characters:** n/a

265. *Traces* by Paula Fox. A number of animals leave their tracks across the land. Genre: natural science

Pace: deliberate **Tone:** hopeful* **Story Line:** plot twists* **Characters:** quirky
> 266. *The Treasure* by Uri Shulevitz. Following a dream, a poor old man seeks treasure in the city, only to find it closer to home in the end. Genre: folktale-like

Pace: deliberate **Tone:** humorous* **Story Line:** episodic **Characters:** recognizable
> 267. *Trouble Gum* by Matthew Cordell. Reuben and Julius (two piglets) chew gum, play with it, and blow bubbles, making a mess despite their mother's repeated warnings. Genre: realistic (if you think of the animals as humans)

Pace: unhurried **Tone:** engaging **Story Line:** resolved ending **Characters:** recognizable
> 268. *True Friends: A Tale from Tanzania* by John Kilaka. Elephant betrays his best friend Rat and has to face the anger of all the other animals. Rat's ultimate forgiveness of Elephant restores the animals' peaceful coexistence. Genre: folktale

Pace: easy **Tone:** engaging **Story Line:** engaging **Characters:** recognizable
> 269. *The Twelve Dancing Princesses* by Isadora Rachel. Every night, twelve princesses manage to escape their locked chamber to dance with twelve princes—until their secret is discovered. Genre: fairy tale

Pace: measured **Tone:** mystical* **Story Line:** resolved ending/thought provoking **Characters:** dramatic
> 270. *Twenty Heartbeats* by Dennis Haseley. After decades of waiting for a painting of his favorite horse to be completed, a wealthy man angrily confronts the artist he paid to paint it—only to discover how very hard the painter had been working all those years. Genre: folktale like

Pace: measured **Tone:** engaging **Story Line:** inspirational* **Characters:** lifelike
> 271. *Twenty-one Elephants* by Phil Bidner. An eight-year-old girl (determined to prove to her father that the newly opened Brooklyn Bridge is safe to cross) enlists P. T. Barnum and his elephants to walk across the structure. Genre: historical/realistic

Pace: measured **Tone:** quiet **Story Line:** episodic **Characters:** n/a
> 272. *Twilight Comes Twice* by Ralph Fletcher. Twice each day (at dawn and dusk) twilight arrives. The special magic of each of these times of day is conveyed through poetic prose. Genre: verse/natural science

Pace: lively **Tone:** menacing* **Story Line:** action oriented* **Characters:** well drawn
> 273. *Two Bad Ants* by Chris Van Allsburg. Straying from their group, two bad ants are lucky to live through a series of dangerous misadventures. Genre: animal story

Pace: engrossing **Tone:** engaging **Story Line:** character centered **Characters:** recognizable
> 274. *The Umbrella Queen* by Yim Shirin Bridges. Breaking from her family's and village's tradition of painting only flowers and butterflies on umbrellas, Noot remains true to herself by painting elephants instead. Genre: folktale like

Pace: engrossing **Tone:** bittersweet **Story Line:** family centered/domestic* **Characters:** vivid
> 275. *Uncle Jed's Barber Shop* by Margaree Mitchell King. Despite numerous setbacks, Sarah's uncle Jed finally opens a barber shop after years of being the only black traveling barber in the county. Genre: historical/realistic

Pace: unhurried **Tone:** bittersweet/heartwarming **Story Line:** family centered/fact filled* **Characters:** lifelike
> 276. *Uncle Peter's Amazing Chinese Wedding* by Lenore Look. On Uncle Peter's wedding day, Jenny struggles with "losing" her favorite uncle to his new bride. Note: Ancient as well as modern Chinese wedding customs are scattered throughout the story. Genre: realistic

Pace: compelling/engrossing* **Tone:** suspenseful/hopeful **Story Line:** action oriented/inspirational **Characters:** multiple points of view
> 277. *Under the Quilt of Night* by Deborah Hopkinson. A family of runaway slaves travels the Underground Railroad to freedom. Genre: historical

Pace: unhurried **Tone:** melodramatic* **Story Line:** issue oriented **Characters:** recognizable
278. *Unlovable* by Dan Yaccarino. Alfred the pug thinks of himself as unlovable until he is lucky enough to befriend another pug. Genre: realistic (if you think of the animals as humans)

Pace: easy **Tone:** detailed setting* **Story Line:** episodic **Characters:** lifelike
279. *Uptown* by Bryan Collier. A young boy describes his Harlem neighborhood using imagery. Genre: realistic

Pace: unhurried **Tone:** magical **Story Line:** action oriented **Characters:** vivid
280. *Urso Brunov and the White Emperor* by Brian Jacques. Urso Brunov (the father of all bears) rescues two lost polar bears and (with the help of a number of friends) helps them get back to the Land of Rainbow Lights. Genre: fantasy

Pace: engrossing **Tone:** melodramatic* **Story Line:** character centered **Characters:** quirky
281. *Victor and Christabel* by Petra Mathers. A painting of a sick, sad young woman appears in a museum, where the guard falls in love with the girl and eventually liberates her from the evil spell she was under. Genre: romance/magical realism

Pace: measured **Tone:** bittersweet **Story Line:** event oriented **Characters:** introspective*/realistic
282. *Visiting Day* by Jacqueline Woodson. A young girl looks forward to traveling with her grandmother to visit her father in prison. Genre: realistic/problem

Pace: deliberate **Tone:** bittersweet/psychological **Story Line:** issue oriented*/fact filled **Characters:** realistic
283. *Waiting for Benjamin: A Story About Autism* by Alexandra Jessup Altman. A young boy learns to come to terms with his little brother's autism and the feelings he has regarding his brother's behaviors. Genre: realistic/problem

Pace: stately **Tone:** bittersweet **Story Line:** family centered/thought provoking **Characters:** introspective*
284. *The Wall* by Eve Bunting. A young boy and his father visit the Vietnam War Memorial looking for Grandpa's name on the wall. Genre: realistic

Pace: unhurried* **Tone:** quiet **Story Line:** action oriented **Characters:** realistic
285. *Water Hole Waiting* by Jane and Christopher Kurtz. A small monkey waits for all the other animals to drink at the watering hole before it is safe for him to do so. Genre: natural science

Pace: relaxed **Tone:** quiet* **Story Line:** family centered **Characters:** realistic
286. *The Wednesday Surprise* by Eve Bunting. As a surprise birthday present for her father, Anna teaches her grandma how to read. Genre: realistic

Pace: fast **Tone:** humorous **Story Line:** domestic/family centered **Characters:** recognizable*
287. *When Charlie McButton Lost Power* by Suzanne Collins. When Charlie loses power in a blackout and cannot play his beloved computer games, he learns to appreciate his little sister as well as the idea that fun can be had without electricity. Genre: verse/realistic

Pace: deliberate **Tone:** humorous **Story Line:** character centered/resolved ending* **Characters:** recognizable
288. *When Randolph Turned Rotten* by Charise Mericle Harper. Ralph (the beaver) and Ivy (the goose) are best friends, but when Ivy is invited to a sleepover and Ralph isn't, he tries to spoil her fun. In the end, he is sorry for having turned temporarily rotten. Genre: realistic (if you think of the animals as humans)

Pace: fast **Tone:** engaging **Story Line:** character centered **Characters:** familiar
289. *When Sophie Gets Angry—Really, Really Angry . . .* by Molly Bang. Sophie's way of dealing with her anger is to run away, climb a tree, and take a time out for herself. Genre: realistic

Pace: fast **Tone:** humorous **Story Line:** action oriented* **Characters:** quirky
290. *When Turtle Grew Feathers* by Tim Tingle. In this retelling of Aesop's fable, the real reason the turtle won is revealed: Rabbit was not racing a turtle after all. Genre: fable (retold)

Pace: easy **Tone:** humorous/upbeat **Story Line:** resolved ending **Characters:** dramatic/quirky*
> 291. *Who Wants to be a Poodle—I Don't* by Lauren Child. Trixie Twinkle Toes Trot-a-Lot Delight is tired of living the life of a pampered poodle and tries every which way she can think of to convince her owner (Verity Brulee) to let her just be a dog. Genre: animal story

Pace: unhurried **Tone:** engaging **Story Line:** resolved ending **Characters:** dramatic
> 292. *Who's in Rabbit's House? A Retold Masai Tale* by Verna Aardema. A number of animals offer to help Rabbit get an intruder out of her house. Each of them ends up making matters worse until Frog unexpectedly comes to the rescue. Genre: folktale

Pace: fast/lively **Tone:** humorous **Story Line:** gentle **Characters:** recognizable*
> 293. *Why Is the Sky Blue?* by Sally Grindley. Wise, old Donkey comes around to the understanding that there are many ways to learn and that Rabbit's way isn't necessarily all bad. Genre: animal story

Pace: measured **Tone:** bittersweet* **Story Line:** inspirational/thought provoking **Characters:** lifelike
> 294. *Wilfrid Gordon McDonald Partridge* by Mem Fox. A small boy helps an elderly woman "find" her memory. Genre: realistic

Pace: deliberate **Tone:** hopeful/bittersweet **Story Line:** inspirational/thought provoking **Characters:** eccentric*/well drawn
> 295. *Wings* by Christopher Myers. Ikarus Jackson is different. With a little encouragement, he embraces his uniqueness and follows his own heart. Genre: allegory/magical realism

Pace: compelling **Tone:** humorous **Story Line:** episodic* **Characters:** eccentric/well drawn
> 296. *Wolf!* by Becky Bloom. A pig, a duck, and a cow teach a wolf about the importance and joys of being a good reader. Genre: animal story

Pace: engrossing **Tone:** creepy*/suspenseful/foreboding **Story Line:** action oriented **Characters:** quirky
> 297. *The Wolves in the Walls* by Neil Gaiman. When the wolves come out of the walls, Lucy and her family must figure out how to reclaim their home from the invaders. Genre: magical realism

Pace: engrossing **Tone:** dark/heavy **Story Line:** thought provoking*/issue oriented **Characters:** familiar
> 298. *The Wretched Stone* by Chris Van Allsburg. A ship's crew picks up a strange, glowing rock that ends up transforming them from lively and intelligent to hypnotized and beastly. (Think: TV) Genre: allegory

Pace: deliberate **Tone:** foreboding* **Story Line:** issue oriented **Characters:** recognizable
> 299. *The Wump World* by Bill Peet. The Pollutians (from planet Pollutius) invade Wump World and very nearly destroy it completely with overdevelopment. Genre: allegorical tale

Pace: lively **Tone:** melodramatic* **Story Line:** family centered **Characters:** dramatic*
> 300. *Yesterday I Had the Blues* by Jeron Ashford Frame. A young boy thinks about the emotions each of his family members feel and equates each with a different color, from his blues to his father's grays to his grandmother's yellows. Genre: realistic

Pace: leisurely **Tone:** engaging **Story Line:** issue oriented **Characters:** lifelike
> 301. *Yoko* by Rosemary Wells. Yoko's classmates make fun of her sushi lunch until one of them actually tries it and likes it. Genre: realistic (if you think of the animals as humans)

Pace: easy **Tone:** bittersweet **Story Line:** family centered **Characters:** faithful*
> 302. *Yoko's Paper Cranes* by Rosemary Wells. When Yoko moves away from her grandparents in Japan, she reminds them that one day she will return by sending them origami paper cranes she has made. Genre: realistic (if you think of the animals as humans)

Pace: easy **Tone:** humorous **Story Line:** character centered **Characters:** vivid
> 303. *Young Mouse and Elephant—An East African Folktale* by Pamela Farris. Young Mouse is convinced he is the strongest creature on the savannah—stronger even than Elephant. Genre: folktale

Pace: measured **Tone:** foreboding*/suspenseful **Story Line:** issue oriented **Characters:** realistic/recognizable

304. *Your Move* by Eve Bunting. Ten-year-old James thinks he wants to join the K-Bones until his initiation endangers his little brother Isaac and he finds the courage to turn down the invitation to join. Genre: realistic/problem

Pace: unhurried **Tone:** mystical* **Story Line:** mystical* **Characters:** introspective

305. *Zen Ghosts* by Jon J. Muth. On Halloween night, the giant panda Stillwater tells Addy, Michael, and Karl a ghost story that touches on the concept of the duality in all people. Genre: magical realism

Pace: easy **Tone:** engaging **Story Line:** gentle/layered **Characters:** introspective

306. *Zen Ties* by Jon J. Muth. Through the experience of helping a grouchy elderly neighbor, Koo, Addy, Michael, and Karl learn a valuable lesson from Stillwater the panda. Genre: magical realism

Pace: fast **Tone:** engaging **Story Line:** action oriented **Characters:** vivid*

307. *Zomo the Rabbit* by Gerald McDermott. Zomo the rabbit (a trickster) wants wisdom and sets out to achieve the three tasks set before him by Sky God. Genre: trickster tale

*The story/book is best suited to teaching the appeal term to which the * is appended.

Appendix B-7
Book Hooks Without Covers Alphabetical by Title

GET HOOKED ON READING!!

Title: *24 Girls in 7 Days*

Author: Alex Bradley

Genre: Humorous Realistic Fiction

Here's the Hook:

Jack Grammar's love life is nothing short of pathetic. Being a nice guy has not helped him at all. Now senior prom is only 10 days away and Jack has no one to go with. Enter Natalie and Pierce. Using the school's online newspaper and in a stroke of genius, they run an ad for Jack to get a prom date. The comedy begins when 200 girls respond to the ad and Jack has to speed date 24 of them in one week. Get to know Jack better than any one of his 24 dates ever could. Read this funny, heartwarming story about a smart, gentle kid with a huge heart, a fabulous dog named Flip, and more than a couple of unique friends.

Three words or phrases that best describe this book are:
• Humorous tone
• Layered story line
• Well-developed/lovable characters

Name: O. Nesi

GET HOOKED ON READING!!

Title: *The Absolutely True Diary of a Part-Time Indian*

Author: Sherman Alexie

Genre: Humorous Realistic Fiction

Here's the Hook:

Living on the Spokane Indian Reservation, Junior is surrounded by sadness, extreme poverty, racism, alcoholism, and death. What possible chance does he have to make it in the world off the rez, in an all-white high school? The reality is that he will never know if he doesn't try. With the deep love and support of his crazy family, Junior learns to overcome the many obstacles that threaten to keep him down. By turns heartbreakingly sad and laugh-out-loud hilarious, this magical book teaches the only lesson truly worth learning: without hope, there is nothing.

Three words or phrases that best describe this book are:
• Unhurried pace
• Darkly humorous and deeply hopeful tone
• Character-centered story line

Name: O. Nesi

GET HOOKED ON READING!!

Title: *A Drowned Maiden's Hair: A Melodrama*

Author: Laura Amy Schlitz

Genre: Historical Fiction/Mystery

Here's the Hook:

When the orphan child Maud Flynn is adopted by three sisters, she can hardly believe her luck. After all, Maud knows that she is plain, stubborn, and badly behaved besides. What could Victoria, Judith, and Hyacinth possibly see in her to want to rescue her from her horrid life in the Barbary Orphanage? Yet adopt her they do, and gradually Maud discovers the sisters' plan for her: a life of lies lived in hiding and helping them with the family business. Desperate for any bit of love she can get, Maud bears the burden of keeping the family's secrets until she is forced to make a decision that will alter the course of her life forever.

Three words or phrases that best describe this book are:
• Mysterious tone
• Dramatic story line
• Vivid, well-developed characters

Name: O. Nesi

GET HOOKED ON READING!!

Title: *Acceleration*

Author: Graham McNamee

Genre: Mystery/Thriller

Here's the Hook:

Duncan's summer job in the subway's lost and found seems like it's going to be a total bore until he comes across the diary of a psychotic serial killer. Prepare for a rollercoaster ride of creepiness and nail-biting suspense as Duncan and his friends try to track the psycho down before he graduates from torturing and killing animals to torturing and killing people. Alternating between "guy" humor and disturbing glimpses into a twisted mind, this book is completely gripping—a true-adrenaline fueled rocket ride.

Three words or phrases that best describe this book are:
• Compelling pace
• Creepy tone
• Vivid characters
Note: This is an eighth-grade book.

Name: O. Nesi

GET HOOKED ON READING!!	GET HOOKED ON READING!!
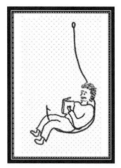	

Title: *After Tupac & D Foster*

Author: Jacqueline Woodson

Genre: Realistic Fiction

Here's the Hook:

Out of nowhere, D Foster shows up in the lives of Neeka and her best friend. Living in foster care and wise beyond her years, D Foster reaches into the very souls of her new friends. Slowly, quietly and steadily she makes her deep impact on their lives. With Tupac's life and music unfolding in the background, this powerful, sensitive, and emotional story about friendship and growing up keeps readers thinking long after the book is done.

Three words or phrases that best describe this book are:
• Unhurried pace
• Bittersweet tone
• Character-centered story line

Name: O. Nesi

Title: *The Alchemyst: The Secrets of the Immortal Nicholas Flamel*

Author: Michael Scott

Genre: Fantasy

Here's the Hook:

From the first page to the last, nonstop action drives this book at a breakneck pace. Two fifteen-year-old twins (Josh and Sophie) learn that the fate of the world rests in their hands. Packed with head-spinning battles between good and evil forces, the story line unfolds in dizzying swirls. Magic, shape shifting, auras, alchemy, and superhuman powers catapult these unlikely heroes through a series of fantastical events. Prepare for a reading roller coaster ride.

Three words or phrases that best describe this book are:
• Breakneck pace
• Mysterious/magical tone
• Action-packed story line

Name: O. Nesi

GET HOOKED ON READING!!

Title: *All Shook Up*

Author: Shelley Pearsall

Genre: Humorous Realistic Fiction

Here's the Hook:

Josh does not have it easy. Or so he thinks, anyway. To hear him tell it, his life is a disaster. His parents are divorced and living states apart from each other. He keeps getting bounced back and forth between Chicago and Boston. If all this weren't bad enough, he is shipped off to live with his Dad for a while and learns that his father has lost his job as a shoe salesman and become a full-time Elvis impersonator. How totally embarrassing! What if his new school-mates find out? Where will he go to hide from the ridicule? By turns bittersweet and laugh-out-loud funny, this story is both realistic and heart-warming.

Three words or phrases that best describe this book are:
• Easy pace
• Engaging tone
• Gentle story line

Name: O. Nesi

GET HOOKED ON READING!!

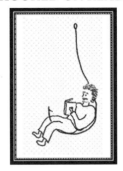

Title: *All the Lovely Bad Ones*

Author: Mary Downing Hahn

Genre: Ghost Story

Here's the Hook:

What exactly happened at the Fox Hill Inn all those many years ago that causes it to be haunted now? And why do Travis and Corey's pranks bring the ghosts back out of their graves after years of silence? What will the brother and sister have to do to send the ghosts back to where they came from, and will they have the courage to do it? Repeated hauntings by the ghosts gradually reveal the pain and suffering inflicted at the site until the living can no longer ignore the ghosts' demands for revenge and peace in death.

Three words or phrases that best describe this book are:
• Deliberate pace
• Spooky tone
• Action-oriented story line

Name: O. Nesi

GET HOOKED ON READING!!

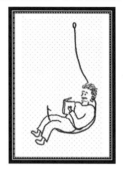

Title: *At the Sign of the Sugared Plum*

Author: Mary Hooper

Genre: Historical Fiction

Here's the Hook:

Travel back to London in 1665—the year the city was struck by the plague and 100,000 of its 300,000 citizens died of the disease. Full of historical details both fascinating and gruesome, this novel tells the story of fifteen-year-old Hannah and her older sister Sarah. Their daily struggles to remain free of the plague make for both gripping and horrifying reading. Learn about death pits, apothecaries, enclosed homes, and some of the crazy cures people thought would help them fight the Plague—all as you sit at the edge of your seat, wondering: will Hannah and Sarah escape London alive, or will the Plague devour them as it did so many others?

Three words or phrases that best describe this book are:
• Fast pace
• Suspenseful tone
• Gripping story line

Name: O. Nesi

GET HOOKED ON READING!!

Title: *Barb and Dingbat's Crybaby Hotline*

Author: Patrick Jennings

Genre: Humorous Realistic Fiction

Here's the Hook:

Jeff likes girls and they like him. In fact, he's as popular as a guy can get in junior high. So why did his girlfriend Viv get her friend Barb to call him to dump him? And why isn't Barb like all the other girls in his school? She doesn't like him at all and makes no effort to hide the fact. Through a series of hilarious phone conversations between Barb and Jeff, readers get a true to life glimpse of the workings of junior high school in the 1970s.

Three words or phrases that best describe this book are:
• Fast pace/quick read
• Humorous/sarcastic tone
• Realistic characters

Name: O. Nesi

GET HOOKED ON READING!!

Title: *The Black Book of Secrets*

Author: F. E. Higgins

Genre: Fantasy/Mystery

Here's the Hook:

From its nail-bitingly tense opening scene to its magical conclusion, this book takes hold and never lets go for an instant. Enter the life of young Ludlow Fitch as he becomes the apprentice of Joe Zabbidou, Secret Pawnbroker. Hear the dark confessions of the gravedigger, the butcher, and the book and coffin makers, each whispered at midnight to Joe in the back room of his pawn shop in the town of Pagus Parvus and recorded by Ludlow in *The Black Book of Secrets*. And what of Jeremiah Ratchet, the greedy, greasy landlord of many of the townspeople of Pagus Parvus? In this gripping tale, all is revealed in due and proper time.

Three words or phrases that best describe this book are:
• Measured/driving pace
• Darkly magical tone
• Vivid characters

Name: O. Nesi

GET HOOKED ON READING!!

Title: *Bonechiller*

Author: Graham McNamee

Genre: Psychological Horror

Here's the Hook:

In the dead of a dark, icy-cold Canadian winter, in the small town of Harvest Cove, teenagers have been disappearing mysteriously. Tension and suspense build gradually in this relentlessly eerie novel as the main characters figure out that the town's teens are being stalked and ultimately killed by a windigo—a huge, demonic, literally bone-chilling wild beast. Desperate to be free of this creature and its evil, the teens devise a plan to exterminate it. Whether they succeed depends entirely on the extent of their bravery and willingness to face down a terrifying enemy.

Three words or phrases that best describe this book are:
• Compelling pace
• Dark, creepy tone
• Action-oriented story line

Name: O. Nesi

GET HOOKED ON READING!!	**GET HOOKED ON READING!!**

Title: *The Book of Dead Days*	**Title:** *Born to Rock*
Author: Marcus Sedgwick	**Author:** Gordon Korman
Genre: Magical Realism/Historical Fiction	**Genre:** Humorous Realistic Fiction
Here's the Hook:	**Here's the Hook:**
It is the second half of the eighteenth century (in the days between Christmas and New Year's), and Valerian (a magician and practitioner of the "dark arts") is desperate to find a way out of the pact with evil he made fifteen years earlier. With his assistant Boy in tow, he sets off on a spine-tingling, suspenseful, and tension-filled journey through the city's cemeteries and dark underground waterways in search of the Book of Dead Days—where Valerian is convinced he will find the answer to breaking the pact and free himself of the death sentence that will otherwise be visited upon him on New Year's Day.	When a misunderstanding derails Leo's plans to attend Harvard University on a scholarship, he is forced to reach out to his biological father: Marion X. McMurphy (AKA King Maggot, the lead singer of the punk rock band Purge). Told from Leo's point of view, and laced with sarcasm, one comical situation after another unfolds until Leo finds himself on the wrong side of the law and with greater knowledge about himself, his true father, and his friends than he ever intended to have.
Three words or phrases that best describe this book are: • Compelling pace • Dark/creepy tone • Action-oriented story line	**Three words or phrases that best describe this book are:** • Humorous tone • Character-centered story line • Well-developed characters **Note:** This is an eighth-grade book.
Name: O. Nesi	**Name:** O. Nesi

GET HOOKED ON READING!!

Title: *The Boy From the Basement*

Author: Susan Shaw

Genre: Realistic Fiction/Problem Novel

Here's the Hook:

For as long as he can remember, twelve-year-old Charlie has lived in the basement as punishment for being bad. No clothes for Charlie except for a pair of old shorts. No bed, no blanket, just an old, filthy towel. No school, no outdoors, no life. No food or water all day until he is able to sneak into the kitchen at night and scrounge what little he can that Father won't notice is missing. Long after he is free of the basement and his never-ending punishment, Charlie's painful story of abuse continues to imprison him in a state of near-constant fear.

Three words or phrases that best describe this book are:
• Deliberate/measured pace
• Bleak/fearful tone
• Character-centered/psychological story line

Name: O. Nesi

GET HOOKED ON READING!!

Title: *Brooklyn Bridge*

Author: Karen Hesse

Genre: Historical Fiction

Here's the Hook:

Full of fascinating historical details, this novel takes readers back to the summer of 1903. The family of fourteen-year-old Joseph Michtom invents the stuffed teddy bear, and his life changes forever. There is no more free time to play stickball with the guys, and there is certainly not any time for Joseph to visit Coney Island—the one thing he wants to do most. It's all work all the time as the family struggles to survive in turn-of-the-century immigrant Brooklyn. Their lives, however, seem positively wonderful compared to those of the homeless runaway children who live under the Brooklyn Bridge and who are regularly haunted by a child ghost.

Three words or phrases that best describe this book are:
• Unhurried pace
• Story line has multiple plotlines
• Well-developed characters

Name: O. Nesi

GET HOOKED ON READING!!	GET HOOKED ON READING!!

Title: *Canned*

Author: Alex Shearer

Genre: Mystery

Here's the Hook:

Surely cans without labels contain the same stuff as cans with labels: corn, soup, dog food, beans . . . right? The only difference must be that they don't have labels . . . or is it? What if some cans without labels turn out to contain parts of a mystery? If you collected these cans and discovered clues to solve a mystery, how far would you go to solve it? Join Fergal and Charlotte in this roller coaster ride of a novel as their can collections gradually reveal bits and pieces (literally) of a gruesome mystery. Mounting suspense and tension lead to a thrilling conclusion.

Note: This novel is set in England.

Three words or phrases that best describe this book are:
• Engrossing pace
• Suspenseful tone
• Quirky/unique characters

Name: O. Nesi

Title: *The Case of the Missing Marquess: An Enola Holmes Mystery*

Author: Nancy Springer

Genre: Historical Fiction/Mystery

Here's the Hook:

It is not at all surprising that fourteen-year-old Enola Holmes is both clever and stubborn. She is, after all, the much younger sister of the famous Sherlock Holmes. When her mother disappears, Enola is not about to follow Sherlock's order that she must go live in an orphanage. Off to solve the mystery of her mother's disappearance, Enola lands square in the middle of a kidnapping case. Down the rat-infested alleys of 1800s London she goes, chasing and being chased by both kidnappers and Scotland Yard detectives.

Three words or phrases that best describe this book are:
• Fast pace
• Suspenseful tone
• Action-oriented story line

Name: O. Nesi

GET HOOKED ON READING!!

Title: *Chains*

Author: Laurie Halse Anderson

Genre: Historical Fiction

Here's the Hook:

Despite being promised their freedom, twelve-year-old Isabel and her five-year-old sister Ruth are sold off to slave owners living in New York City during Revolutionary War times. Told from the Isabel's point of view, this story is full of fascinating historical details that paint an accurate picture of what life was like at the time for a young slave girl. Emotional, extremely moving, and totally engaging, this novel pulls the reader in from the very first page. You will feel as though you are living Isabel's life with her.

Three words or phrases that best describe this book are:
• Compelling pace
• Bittersweet tone
• Well-developed characters

Name: O. Nesi

GET HOOKED ON READING!!

Title: *The Chronicles of Vladimir Tod—Eighth Grade Bites*

Author: Heather Brewer

Genre: Contemporary Teen Fantasy

Here's the Hook:

Eighth grade is no picnic for Vlad: he is bullied nonstop, the principal dogs him, and the girl he has a crush on likes his best friend instead. And then there's the fact that his parents are dead, he's a vampire, and his favorite teacher is missing in action. Mr. Otis, the substitute teacher, makes Vlad extremely nervous—he seems to know about Vlad's well-kept vampire secrets. Stalked by an evil vampire killer and desperate to discover Mr. Otis's real intentions, Vlad embarks on a whirlwind of action, unsure who he can trust and who he should be deathly afraid of.

Three words or phrases that best describe this book are:
• Deliberate pace
• Suspenseful tone
• Action-oriented story line

Name: O. Nesi

GET HOOKED ON READING!!

Title: *The Compound*

Author: S. A. Bodeen

Genre: Science Fiction

Here's the Hook:

In this dark, disturbing novel, you are trapped underground with Eli and the Yanakakis family. The compound they live in is huge and was well stocked. They escaped into it following what their father told them was a nuclear war. Six years later, food is running out, and the behaviors of Eli and his sisters are getting weirder and weirder. But if their actions are strange, that's nothing compared to those of their father. How long could you live underground without ever being able to leave? What if you suspected you *could* leave, but your father was preventing you from doing so?

Three words or phrases that best describe this book are:
• Fast paced/tension filled
• Suspenseful/foreboding tone
• Well-developed characters

Name: O. Nesi

GET HOOKED ON READING!!

Title: *Creature of the Night*

Author: Kate Thompson

Genre: Realistic Fiction/Thriller

Here's the Hook:

Bobby sees no future for himself but one in which he and his friends drink, do drugs, and commit crimes to support their various habits. When his abusive and violent mother moves him and his brother to the country, Bobby vows to run away to return to his life in the city. As if he needed any more encouragement to run back to Dublin, the family learns that the house they are living in was the site of several brutal murders. Steadily creeping menace takes over as Bobby becomes desperate to escape the odd and regular nighttime haunting.

Three words or phrases that best describe this book are:
• Creepy, menacing tone
• Violent story line
• Realistic characters

Name: O. Nesi

GET HOOKED ON READING!!

Title: *Cricket Man*

Author: Phyllis Reynolds Naylor

Genre: Realistic Fiction

Here's the Hook:

Seventh grader Kenny Sykes is a thoroughly recognizable character. He's a gentle and kind kid having a somewhat difficult time adjusting to a new school. Determined to save the many crickets and insects that end up floating (near death) in his family's backyard pool, Kenny secretly names himself Cricket Man. Over the same summer, he falls in love with high school junior Jodie Poindexter, who also seems to need saving (though from what, Kenny is unsure). In a completely unexpected and breathtaking plot twist, Kenny finds out precisely how he can save Jodie and does so with genuine heart and deeply moving kindness.

Three words or phrases that best describe this book are:
- Easy pace
- Heartwarming tone
- Character-centered story line

Name: O. Nesi

GET HOOKED ON READING!!

Title: *Deep and Dark and Dangerous*

Author: Mary Downing Hahn

Genre: Ghost Story

Here's the Hook:

Sycamore Lake is deep, dark, and dangerous. The weather in Maine is cold, rainy, and gloomy, and the family cabin is surrounded by trees and often, fog. Ali vacations at the cabin in the hopes of getting an answer to her questions: Who was the third girl in that picture of her mom and her Aunt Dulcie and why was she torn out of the photograph? What, exactly, happened at the lake some thirty years earlier that made the family abandon the cabin? Why does her four-year-old cousin Emma keep dreaming about bones in the lake, and why does Ali keep getting the feeling that something is lurking in the dark corners of the cabin?

Three words or phrases that best describe this book are:
- Unhurried pace
- Spooky/foreboding/menacing tone
- Tense/taut/suspenseful story line

Name: O. Nesi

GET HOOKED ON READING!!

Title: *Defect*

Author: Will Weaver

Genre: Contemporary Teen Fantasy

Here's the Hook:

What if the defect you were born with enabled you to fly? Would you keep it secret, or show it off? Fifteen-year-old David has hidden wings. In addition to having wings, his face is also mis-shapen. With bulging eyes, huge, really sensitive ears, and a taste for eating bugs, how long can David keep his defects from others? And what happens when he decides he doesn't want to hide his true self any more?

Three words or phrases that best describe this book are:
• Engrossing pace
• Inspirational story line
• Magical characters and events

Name: O. Nesi

GET HOOKED ON READING!!

Title: *Defining Dulcie*

Author: Paul Acampora

Genre: Realistic Fiction

Here's the Hook:

Dulcie Morrigan Jones is defined by those she loves: her father (who dies in a janitorial accident), her eccentric grandfather Frank, her impulsive mother, and her abused friend Roxanne. As this cast of unusual secondary characters interacts with her, Dulcie finds the strength and wisdom to begin her life anew.

Three words or phrases that best describe this book are:
• Quick pace
• Heartening/satisfying tone
• Character-/emotion-driven story line

Name: O. Nesi

GET HOOKED ON READING!!

GET HOOKED ON READING!!

Title: *Donuthead*

Author: Sue Stauffacher

Genre: Realistic Fiction

Here's the Hook:

Franklin Delano Donuthead is miserable—and not only because of his name. Completely neurotic, Franklin lives in constant fear that disease and death are everywhere, just waiting to attack him. When his sanitary world is turned upside down by unhygienic Sarah Kervick, Franklin struggles mightily to adjust. Being carefree is not in Franklin's personality, and worrying is not at all in Sarah's. The emotional battles between these two characters are often funny and always moving.

Three words or phrases that best describe this book are:
• Humorous tone
• Quirky characters
• Emotional story line

Name: O. Nesi

Title: *Eggs*

Author: Jerry Spinelli

Genre: Realistic Fiction

Here's the Hook:

Nine-year-old David's mother is dead. Thirteen-year-old Primrose's mother is a fortunetelling crackpot. David wants nothing more than to have his mother back. To get away from *her* mother, Primrose moves out of the house and into an old van parked on the front lawn. As an unlikely friendship develops between these two characters, their innermost secrets and deepest emotions are revealed.

Three words or phrases that best describe this book are:
• Unhurried pace
• Bittersweet/quiet tone
• Character-driven story line

Name: O. Nesi

GET HOOKED ON READING!!

Title: *Emma-Jean Lazarus Fell Out of a Tree*

Author: Lauren Tarshis

Genre: Realistic Fiction

Here's the Hook:

Seventh grader Emma-Jean Lazarus is extremely smart and also very strange (in all the best possible ways). Being smart and strange in middle school, however, is not exactly easy. None of her classmates understands how she thinks. Nor does she understand how they think. Full of quirky, well-developed, and extremely realistic and relatable middle school characters, this story is all about being true to oneself in the face of peer pressure and about finding ways to listen to one's own heart.

Three words or phrases that best describe this book are:
• Deliberate pace
• Heartwarming tone
• Gentle/character-centered story line

Name: O. Nesi

GET HOOKED ON READING!!

Title: *Exit Point*

Author: Laura Langston

Genre: Contemporary Teen Fantasy/Problem Novel

Here's the Hook:

Every life has an exit point. Logan was supposed to "exit" his life at age 77 (at exit point 5). At sixteen years old, however, he makes a bad decision and ends up exiting his life at point 2. This novel is a thought-provoking look at the idea that our actions deeply affect the lives of others. Frantic to fix some part of what he broke by exiting his life too soon, Logan struggles to face his own shortcomings and help those he left behind deal with his death.

Three words or phrases that best describe this book are:
• Compelling pace
• Bittersweet tone
• Thought-provoking story line

Name: O. Nesi

GET HOOKED ON READING!!	**GET HOOKED ON READING!!**

<table>
<tr>
<td>

Title: *Eye of the Crow—The Boy Sherlock Holmes. His 1st Case*

Author: Shane Peacock

Genre: Historical Fiction Mystery

Here's the Hook:

A beautiful young woman is found murdered in the back alley of a London slum in the year 1867. A young butcher's assistant is arrested for the crime and set to hang for it as well. Thirteen-year-old Sherlock Holmes knows the murder was committed by someone else entirely. Feel the thrill of sneaking with Sherlock into the homes of those he suspects of having committed the murder. Follow Sherlock into the dark, twisting, suffocating alleys of London as he solves his first case.

Three words or phrases that best describe this book are:
• Compelling pace
• Suspenseful tone
• Well-developed characters and setting

Name: O. Nesi

</td>
<td>

Title: *Fever 1793*

Author: Laurie Halse Anderson

Genre: Historical Fiction

Here's the Hook:

The year is 1793, and the city of Philadelphia is in the grips of a terrifying yellow fever epidemic. Thousands of citizens are dying both from the fever and from the cures doctors at the time thought would heal them. Travel back in time to the life of fifteen-year-old Mattie Cook, a typical teenager of the day. Turn the pages of this gripping novel and learn what becomes of her and her family when the yellow fever epidemic hits their lives, destroying nearly everything in its path.

Three words or phrases that best describe this book are:
• Engrossing pace
• Suspenseful tone
• Well-developed characters
Note: This book is similar in tone and feel to *At the Sign of the Sugared Plum.*

Name: O. Nesi

</td>
</tr>
</table>

Title: *Funerals & Fly Fishing*

Author: Mary Bartek

Genre: Realistic Fiction

Here's the Hook:

You try living with the last name Stanislawski and see how much you like it. I bet you don't like it at all—and neither does Brad. The difference is, he's stuck with the name, and he's also stuck spending the summer with his grandfather (who he's never even met and who owns a funeral home and just happens to be an undertaker). By turns funny and gently thoughtful, the author gradually paints a familiar story of family relationships and of a young character learning to be comfortable living in his own skin—with his own long name, his odd but gentle grandfather, and his quirky mother.

Three words or phrases that best describe this book are:
• Leisurely pace
• Heartwarming tone
• Lifelike/realistic characters and situations

Name: O. Nesi

GET HOOKED ON READING!!

Title: *Good Enough*

Author: Paula Yoo

Genre: Humorous Realistic Fiction

Here's the Hook:

There's no question that Patti Yoon's parents love her, but the pressure they put on her to be "the best" is extreme. After all, being a PKD (Perfect Korean Daughter) is, in reality, impossible—or at least insanely difficult—especially once Patti becomes way more interested in Cute Trumpet Guy than in scoring a 2300 on the SATs, being lead violinist in the all-state orchestra, and getting into a top university. By turns hilarious and heartbreaking, this novel takes a close look at how one teenager copes with stress and the pressures created by parents who constantly push her to overachieve. It's a lighthearted look at a heavy subject.

Three words or phrases that best describe this book are:
• Fast paced fun
• Character-centered story line
• Well-developed family situation/characters

Name: O. Nesi

GET HOOKED ON READING!!

Title: *The Graveyard Book*

Author: Neil Gaiman

Genre: Fantasy

Here's the Hook:

A family is brutally murdered. Only the baby escapes alive and ends up in a graveyard being raised by the dead. With several guardians looking out for him, Bod (short for Nobody) learns the ways of the deceased: seeing in the dark, walking through walls, vanishing when necessary. The small world of the graveyard and the love of his companions is more than enough for Bod until the day when it is no longer enough and he must learn to live among the living rather than among the dead.

Three words or phrases that best describe this book are:
• Unhurried pace
• Dark tone
• Mystical story line

Name: O. Nesi

GET HOOKED ON READING!!

Title: *Happy Kid*

Author: Gail Gauthier

Genre: Humorous Realistic Fiction

Here's the Hook:

" 'Bert P. Trotts Middle School is the gateway to hell.' How are you going to fix that?" (Gauthier, 7). Starting seventh grade is not easy, especially not when your mother thinks a self-help book will help you make friends and change your generally negative outlook. Welcome to Kyle's world, a place where his sister teases him mercilessly, his friends stop hanging out with him, and the school's biggest bully wants to be his best bud. How is a book going to help fix all that? One humorous misadventure follows another as Kyle navigates the horrors of seventh grade at Bert P. Trotts and learns that maybe the place isn't as hellish as he first thought.

Three words or phrases that best describe this book are:
• Easy pace
• Light/humorous tone
• Recognizable characters

Name: O. Nesi

GET HOOKED ON READING!!	**GET HOOKED ON READING!!**

Title: *Home, and Other Big, Fat Lies*

Author: Jill Wolfson

Genre: Realistic Fiction/Problem Novel

Here's the Hook:

Whitney (AKA Termite) can't help it if she's lived in twelve foster homes in ten years, nor can she help it if she is a jumpy, smart-mouthed, small-for-her-age ball of constant, sparking energy. With an edgy and darkly humorous tone that perfectly captures Termite's constant hyper-activity and her "all over the map" thinking, readers are given a glimpse into many of the painful issues faced by foster kids moving from home to home.

Plot details take a back seat to the full development of a true-to-life character struggling with making her own unique way through life.

Three words or phrases that best describe this book are:
• Psychological/internal tone
• Character-centered story line
• Quirky, well-developed main character

Name: O. Nesi

Title: *Houdini: The Handcuff King*

Authors: Jason Lutes & Nick Bertozzi

Genre: Graphic Biography

Here's the Hook:

With strikingly drawn comic book-format illustrations, readers time travel back to 1908 to witness Houdini's jump off the Harvard Bridge into the freezing waters of the Charles River. He is tightly handcuffed by both his hands and feet and wrapped in chains. A huge crowd has gathered to watch the amazing Houdini. How will he ever escape? As he plunges into the icy waters below, the suspense and tension mount in the audience. Readers, however, have been let in on the secret of his daring escape.

Three words or phrases that best describe this book are:
• Fast pace
• Suspenseful tone
• Character-centered story line

Name: O. Nesi

Title: *How Angel Peterson Got His Name*

Author: Gary Paulsen

Genre: Humorous Memoir

Here's the Hook:

In a whirlwind of nonstop, hair-raising action, Gary Paulsen takes readers back to his boyhood in Minnesota in the late 1940s. "Boys will be boys" no matter what the year, so make way for Paulsen and his friends to entertain you with unbelievable stories of the variety of insane stunts that nearly got them killed at the age of thirteen. A small sampling includes: being pulled on skis by a car going seventy-four miles per hour, jumping a bike through a hoop of fire, wrestling a bear, and hang gliding with an army surplus kite. Be amazed—but whatever you do, don't try these stunts at home!

Three words or phrases that best describe this book are:
• Fast pace
• Humorous tone
• Episodic story line (one story for each stunt)

Name: O. Nesi

Title: *How the Hangman Lost His Heart*

Author: K. M. Grant

Genre: Humorous Historical Fiction/Adventure

Here's the Hook:

The trouble and adventures begin on the very first page of this rollercoaster ride of a book. Dan Skinslicer (the hangman) feels badly for Alice and, against his better judgment, gets involved in a wild scheme she comes up with to rescue her Uncle Frank's head from the top of Temple Bar (where Dan had to put it on display after hanging, beheading, and drawing and quartering Uncle Frank). With every soldier in London hot on their trail, Dan, Alice, Uncle Frank's severed head, and a full cast of loony characters take off chasing and being chased through England in the year 1746. Hang on!

Three words or phrases that best describe this book are:
• Fast/action-packed pace
• Darkly humorous tone
• Well-developed characters

Name: O. Nesi

GET HOOKED ON READING!!

Title: *Huge*

Author: Sasha Paley

Genre: Realistic Fiction

Here's the Hook:

Told from multiple points of view, this light, entertaining read is the story of two very different girls thrown together as roommates at sleepaway "Fat Camp." April can't wait to get to Wellness Canyon and start losing weight. In fact, she saved for a year to be able to go. Her roommate Wil intends to get back at her super wealthy parents for sending her by actually gaining weight. The drama is cranked up further when both girls develop a crush on Colin. In a resolved ending, both April and Wil learn that friendship is more important than anything else.

Three words or phrases that best describe this book are:
• Easy pace
• Light tone
• Character-centered story line

Name: O. Nesi

GET HOOKED ON READING!!

Title: *Hugging the Rock*

Author: Susan Taylor Brown

Genre: Realistic Fiction/Verse

Here's the Hook:

Rachel does not think she will ever be able to forgive her Mom for running away from home and leaving her behind to live with her Father, who is a rock: silent, tough, impossible to reach. Over time, the day comes when she learns he is none of those things and, painful as it may be, she is actually glad her Mom left.

Three words or phrases that best describe this book are:
• Calm/realistic pace
• Gentle/quiet tone
• Emotional story line
Note: This book is similar in tone and pace to *Pieces of Georgia*, *Love That Dog*, *After Tupac and D. Foster*, and *Minn and Jake*.

Name: O. Nesi

GET HOOKED ON READING!!	**GET HOOKED ON READING!!**

<table>
<tr>
<td>

Title: *The Hunger Games*

Author: Suzanne Collins

Genre: Science Fiction

Here's the Hook:

It is the distant future. The United States has become Panem and the states have been replaced by twelve districts. The population of Panem lives in constant fear of its government. Starvation and violence are the norm. To insure that people remain fearful of the government, each year, every district must send one boy and one girl between the ages of twelve and eighteen to Panem's Hunger Games, where the children will engage in a televised fight to the death. In this page-turning novel, readers bear witness to one of these gruesome hunger games—fight by fight and death by death. Throughout, tension and suspense build—right up to the cliffhanger ending.

Three words or phrases that best describe this book are:
- Breakneck pace
- Dark, fearful tone
- Action-packed story line

Note: This book is similar in tone to *Unwind* by Neal Schusterman

Name: O. Nesi

</td>
<td>

Title: *Hurricane Song*

Author: Paul Volponi

Genre: Realistic Fiction

Here's the Hook:

In this bleak account of the aftereffects of Hurricane Katrina, readers are trapped with Miles and his father in the sweltering, stench-ridden Super Dome in New Orleans. Adding further to the pain and sadness of the story is the fact that Miles and his father do not get along. Miles cannot shake the feeling that his dad loves his jazz music far more than he loves him. Gradually, a picture of human suffering, racial tensions, and unspeakably awful behavior is painted. The only thing rising above the horror of the situation is the human ability to hope in the face of despair.

Three words or phrases that best describe this book are:
- Deliberate pace
- Bleak/stark tone
- Well-developed characters

Name: O. Nesi

</td>
</tr>
</table>

GET HOOKED ON READING!!

Title: *If I Grow Up*

Author: Todd Strasser

Genre: Realistic Fiction/Problem Novel

Here's the Hook:

Follow DeShawn's life from twelve to twenty-eight years old—growing up in the projects in poverty and surrounded by gangs, drugs, and random, brutal violence. Each day brings more unraveled lives, greater problems, and feelings of entrapment. With a hopeless tone throughout, this is the story of a young man who ultimately gives in to his surroundings, accepts his bleak fate and resigns himself to living the role he has been assigned by society.

Three words or phrases that best describe this book are:
• Unhurried pace
• Gritty, sad, hopeless tone
• Recognizable characters

Name: O. Nesi

GET HOOKED ON READING!!

Title: *If I Stay*

Author: Gayle Forman

Genre: Realistic Fiction

Here's the Hook:

Emotional and deeply moving, this is the story of sixteen-year-old Mia, the only survivor of a car crash in which her entire family dies. As her badly injured body lies in a coma in the intensive care unit of a hospital, her "soul" tells the story of her life. The present is gently woven throughout as Mia struggles mightily to make the hardest choice of her entire young life.

Three words or phrases that best describe this book are:
• Engrossing pace
• Deeply bittersweet tone
• Episodic story line (alternating between Mia's past life with her family and her present one in the hospital)

Name: O. Nesi

GET HOOKED ON READING!!

Title: *I'm Exploding Now*

Author: Sid Hite

Genre: Humorous Realistic Fiction

Here's the Hook:

Max Whooten is miserable and convinced he's cursed to boot. All he's ever able to see is the dark side of life: "I watched the news for a while after Dad left. I counted two wars, four murders, one sex scandal, two corporate corruptions, one natural disaster, and a brand new disease. Same old stuff. The only thing missing was a baby kidnapping . . . Sure looks to me like the world is going down the toilet " (Hite 20–21). His idea is that the meaning of life is "there is no meaning, except you have to suffer. Plus you meet a lot of morons along the way" (Hite, 60). Does Max survive the most boring summer ever?

Three words or phrases that best describe this book are:
• Fast paced
• Sarcastic/humorous tone
• Well-developed main character

Name: O. Nesi

GET HOOKED ON READING!!

Title: *Invisible*

Author: Pete Hautman

Genre: Realistic Fiction

Here's the Hook:

Doug Hanson (the "freak") is continually picked on at school. The girl of his dreams calls him a worm. Trying desperately to escape, he becomes obsessed with building an elaborate model railroad and bridge in his basement. He and his only friend Andy talk about everything—except what happened at the Tuttle place a few years back. The long, painful days pass until reality crashes into Doug's life, turning it completely upside-down.

Three words or phrases that best describe this book are:
• Unhurried pace
• Psychological/tense tone
• Character-driven story line

Name: O. Nesi

GET HOOKED ON READING!!

Title: *Joe Rat*

Author: Mark Barratt

Genre: Mystery/Historical Fiction

Here's the Hook:

In the filthy, stench-filled sewers of Victorian London, orphaned Joe crawls around scavenging for scraps worth selling for pennies. He trusts no one and lives a life of utter loneliness in the middle of the overcrowded, dirty city. The course of his days takes a sudden turn for mystery and adventure when he meets up with a runaway girl and a "madman." In this gritty, dark novel, a chilling tale of deep misery unfolds at a completely engaging pace. A number of plot twists keep the pages turning.

Three words or phrases that best describe this book are:
• Compelling pace
• Foreboding, dark, gritty tone
• Action-driven story line

Name: O. Nesi

GET HOOKED ON READING!!

Title: *Joyride*

Author: Amy Ehrlich

Genre: Realistic Fiction/Problem Novel

Here's the Hook:

Over time, Nina has grown accustomed to moving once a year, starting in new schools every year, and struggling to make new friends each time. What she cannot get used to is the loneliness and isolation in her life. It's just her and her mother, constantly on the move, from one end of the country to the other, then back again. But now Nina is in the eighth grade and tired of moving so much. Why can't she and her mother ever stay in one place? Why can't she have a more normal life? What secrets is her mother keeping from her?

In this deeply emotional novel, a young girl struggles to understand her mother's moods and unpredictability. An unexpected plot twist reveals the true reason for their constant moving around. Nothing, however, is resolved by this knowledge.

Three words or phrases that best describe this book are:
• Measured pace
• Bleak, sad tone
• Emotionally unresolved ending

Name: O. Nesi

GET HOOKED ON READING!!

Title: *The Juvie Three*

Author: Gordon Korman

Genre: Realistic Fiction/Problem Novel

Here's the Hook:

Gecko, Terence, and Arjay are each doing time in different juvenile detention facilities when Douglas Healy shows up to take the boys to an experimental halfway house he is running in NYC. Having been a juvenile delinquent himself, Mr. Healy is determined to help the boys in any way that he can. When an accident lands him in the hospital with amnesia, the boys figure out a way to stay out of the facilities they were rescued from. The longer Mr. Healy is without a memory, the more the tension and suspense build. Will someone figure out Gecko, Terence, and Arjay are not being supervised? In a whirlwind of action, the boys struggle to keep one step ahead of the law and risk losing their only chance to stay out of juvie.

Three words or phrases that best describe this book are:
• An unhurried pace gives way to a breakneck one in the second half of the book.
• Gritty/hard-edged tone
• Action-oriented story line

Name: O. Nesi

GET HOOKED ON READING!!

Title: *Knucklehead: Tall Tales & Mostly True Stories About Growing Up Scieszka*

Author: Jon Scieszka

Genre: Humorous Memoir

Here's the Hook:

In this humorous memoir, the author of *The Stinky Cheese Man and Other Fairly Stupid Fairy Tales* recounts his childhood growing up with five brothers. No sooner does one of the brothers get his collarbone broken playing football than another one is tied to his bed and yet another digs up the house plants and eats the dirt. Chock full of surprises and knuckleheaded behavior, this memoir creates a vivid picture of nonstop boy action as Jon Scieszka and his brothers run wild, wreck and throw things, and cause constant chaos for Mom and Dad.

Three words or phrases that best describe this book are:
• Very fast pace
• Humorous/light tone
• Episodic story line (one chapter for each knuckleheaded activity)

Name: O. Nesi

GET HOOKED ON READING!!

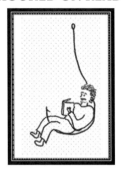

Title: *The Last Apprentice: Revenge of the Witch*

Author: Joseph Delaney

Genre: Fantasy

Here's the Hook:

As the seventh son of a seventh son, Thomas Ward is the last hope of the county. For years, Old Gregory has been the county's Spook, ridding the local villages of evil (capturing witches, binding boggarts, and driving away ghosts). It is time for him to retire. Someone will have to take over his job. Twenty-nine apprentices have tried. Some were too frightened, some fled, some died trying. Thomas is the last apprentice to undertake facing down spine-chilling evil in Chipenden County.

Three words or phrases that best describe this book are:
• Fast pace
• Creepy/dark tone
• Action-oriented story line

Name: O. Nesi

GET HOOKED ON READING!!

Title: *The Last Book in the Universe*

Author: Rodman Philbrick

Genre: Science Fiction

Here's the Hook:

In the distant future, our world is a broken place —polluted, dark, and grimy. No one can read any more, and all books are gone. The only thing "normals" care about is the distraction provided by mind probes. Chaos, starvation, poverty, ignorance, violence, and death rule. Spaz cannot mind probe (due to a brain defect he has). He has no escape from the ugliness of his world, yet he somehow manages to get away and experience a whole different way of living.

Three words or phrases that best describe this book are:
• Deliberate pace
• Dark tone
• Thought-provoking story line
Note: This book is similar in tone to *Unwind* and *The Hunger Games*.

Name: O. Nesi

GET HOOKED ON READING!!

GET HOOKED ON READING!!

Title: *Lawn Boy*

Author: Gary Paulsen

Genre: Humorous Realistic Fiction

Here's the Hook:

How much money do you figure you could make if your loopy grandmother gave you an old riding lawnmower for your birthday? Enough to buy an inner tube for your old ten-speed bike? Would you make fifty dollars? Two hundred dollars? Eight thousand dollars? How about fifty thousand dollars? In this hilarious little book, one twist leads to another, and a twelve-year-old suddenly finds himself involved in way more than he anticipated.

Three words or phrases that best describe this book are:
• Very fast paced
• Very humorous tone
• Story line: full of completely unexpected surprises

Name: O. Nesi

Title: *Lemonade Mouth*

Author: Mark Peter Hughes

Genre: Humorous Realistic Fiction

Here's the Hook:

Freshman year of high school is total torture for Wen, Stella, Charlie, Mohini, and Olivia. Either ridiculed or ignored by the popular kids (and with lousy personal family lives), they just can't win—until the fateful day they all meet each other in after-school detention and end up forming the wild and completely unique band called Lemonade Mouth. Their "weird, emotional, intense music" ends up reaching hundreds upon hundreds of kids in their school, and a revolution is soon on its way. Read each band member's account of how it all happened and prepare yourself for drama, drama, drama!

Three words or phrases that best describe this book are:
• Engrossing pace
• Dramatic tone
• Multiple points of view in characterization

Name: O. Nesi

GET HOOKED ON READING!!

Title: *Leslie's Journal*

Author: Allan Stratton

Genre: Realistic Fiction/Problem novel

Here's the Hook:

The deliberate pace of this novel builds increasing suspense. Leslie's sarcastic, hurtful journal entries fill readers in on the problems she faces in her relationships with her Mom, Dad, best friend Katie, and boyfriend Jason. Angry, untrusting, and vulnerable, Leslie lands in a world of pain from which there is no apparent escape. All the while, the reader is filled with foreboding, knowing that something awful will happen to Leslie unless she can find a way to stop lashing out at the people in her life who truly care about her.

Three words or phrases that best describe this book are:
• Deliberate pace
• Suspenseful tone
• Character-centered story line

Name: O. Nesi

GET HOOKED ON READING!!

Title: *The Liberation of Gabriel King*

Author: K. L. Going

Genre: Realistic Fiction

Here's the Hook:

What are you most afraid of in life? Do you have the courage to confront your fears? What if a friend helped you to face down the things you are most frightened of? The year is 1976, and in a small town in Georgia, Frita Wilson (who is black) has a plan for her best friend Gabe King (who is white and afraid of just about everything) to "get liberated" from his fears. Together they face down spiders, dead bodies, loose cows, and, most terrifying of all, violent racism.

Three words or phrases that best describe this book are:
• Unhurried pace
• Heartwarming/bittersweet tone
• Well-developed characters

Name: O. Nesi

From *Getting Beyond "Interesting": Teaching Students the Vocabulary of Appeal to Discuss Their Reading* by Olga M. Nesi. Santa Barbara, CA: Libraries Unlimited. Copyright © 2012.

GET HOOKED ON READING!!

Title: *Locomotion*

Author: Jacqueline Woodson

Genre: Realistic Fiction

Here's the Hook:

At the age of seven years old, Lonnie Collins Motion (Locomotion) loses both his parents in a horrible fire. Now he is eleven, and his teacher helps him find a way to speak about his pain through the writing of poetry. Sad, smart, and sensitive, Locomotion pulls readers fully into his shattered world—sometimes quietly, sometimes explosively.

Three words or phrases that best describe this book are:
• Unhurried pace
• Gentle/sensitive tone
• Extremely moving story line

Name: O. Nesi

GET HOOKED ON READING!!

Title: *The London Eye Mystery*

Author: Siobhan Dowd

Genre: Mystery

Here's the Hook:

You would never expect a person to disappear off a ferris wheel, would you? Yet that is exactly what happens to Salim. He goes up in the London Eye ferris wheel, and when it completes a full circle, he is no longer on it. His autistic cousin Ted and Ted's older sister Kat decide to try to solve the mystery of Salim's disappearance. Told from Ted's point of view and giving readers a glimpse into the workings of an autistic boy's mind, the suspense builds gradually and in unexpected ways. Ted is certainly unusual but also brilliant, and his ability to see the mystery differently than anyone else does adds much to the quirkiness of this completely engaging mystery.

Three words or phrases that best describe this book are:
• Deliberate pace
• Engaging tone
• Quirky characters

Name: O. Nesi

GET HOOKED ON READING!!

Title: *Looks*

Author: Madeleine George

Genre: Realistic Fiction

Here's the Hook:

Meghan is massive. Aimee is stick thin. Meghan is deeply sad and numb. Aimee is filled with anger and fear. Both are invisible, hiding inside themselves and from those around them, until they find each other and, between them, devise a way to get revenge against the girl who hurt them both.

A carefully controlled pace builds tension throughout this novel, and the reader is deliberately and masterfully put into the minds of each of the story's two main characters. Against a backdrop of bullying and school drama, a deeply emotional story unfolds.

Three words or phrases that best describe this book are:
• Compelling pace
• Psychological tone
• Realistic characters

Name: O. Nesi

GET HOOKED ON READING!!

Title: *Love Among the Walnuts*

Author: Jean Ferris

Genre: Fantasy

Here's the Hook:

Sandy Huntington-Ackerman has lived his entire life away from the horrors of the real world on his family's huge and totally remote estate. Not even the loony bin next door (Walnut Manor) infringes on his dream world. But Sandy's perfect life is shattered when his evil uncles send his parents and their pet chicken (Attila the Hen) into a coma using a poisonous birthday cake. Sandy, his loyal butler, and a wacky nurse are determined to save his parents and find out what's really wrong with the nutty neighbors of Walnut Manor.

Three words or phrase that best describe this book are:

• Magical tone
• Feel-good story line
• Charming/lovable characters

Name: O. Nesi

GET HOOKED ON READING!!

GET HOOKED ON READING!!

Title: *The Magician's Elephant*

Author: Kate DiCamillo

Genre: Fantasy

Here's the Hook:

Is Peter's sister alive? If she is, how can he find her? The fortuneteller spoke of a mysterious elephant—an elephant that would lead him to his long-lost sister. What can the truth possibly be? In this quietly mysterious, gentle, magical little book, follow Peter on his journey to find Adele and meet a cast of quirky and delightful secondary characters. Total escape awaits you in the pages of this novel.

Three words or phrases that best describe this book are:
• Relaxed pace
• Magical tone
• Gentle story line

Name: O. Nesi

Title: *Martyn Pig*

Author: Kevin Brooks

Genre: Realistic Fiction/Problem Novel

Here's the Hook:

In this dark, bleak, and heavy novel, Martyn Pig kills his alcoholic and abusive father in self-defense. Afraid to call the police, he lives with the body in the filthy, squalid, rancid house for four days. In this time, he descends into numbness and emptiness, eventually surrendering to fate and ultimately coming up with a plan to dispose of the body. In a completely breathtaking plot twist, he discovers the true meaning of evil.

Three words or phrases that best describe this book are:
• Relentlessly tense pace
• Dark, gritty, bleak tone
• Twisting story line

Name: O. Nesi

<table>
<tr>
<td>

GET HOOKED ON READING!!

Title: *Maximum Ride—The Angel Experiment*

Author: James Patterson

Genre: Fantasy/Action Adventure

Here's the Hook:

With extremely short chapters, a fast pace, and a high-action story line, the pages of this book practically turn on their own.

Meet Max and her "flock"—six misfit kids who have been genetically mutated to be able to fly. Their escape from the lab is not being taken well by the scientists who created them. Enter the Erasers—other mutant kids designed to be tracking and fighting machines. Their only job now is to bring in Max and the flock—and every time Max thinks she is keeping the flock safe and out of danger, the Erasers show up out of nowhere.

Three words or phrases that best describe this book are:
• Extremely fast pace
• Action-driven story line
• Suspenseful tone

Name: O. Nesi

</td>
<td>

GET HOOKED ON READING!!

Title: *Messed Up*

Author: Janet Nichols Lynch

Genre: Realistic Fiction/Problem Novel

Here's the Hook:

Having to repeat the eighth grade is very nearly the least of RD's problems. His mother is in prison. He does not know his father, and his grandmother has taken off and left him with Earl. When events take a turn for the very worst, RD has to grow up in a hurry. Lost, lonely, and desolate, he slowly learns how to survive. Tired of his friends, of being suspended, of being given detention, and of being viewed as nothing but a troublemaker, he struggles to find his own strength.

Three words or phrases that best describe this book are:
• Urban tone
• Recognizable characters
• Thought provoking story line

Name: O. Nesi

</td>
</tr>
</table>

GET HOOKED ON READING!!

Title: *Middle School is Worse Than Meatloaf—A Year Told Through Stuff*

Author: Jennifer L. Holm

Pictures by: Elicia Castaldi

Genre: Realistic Fiction

Here's the Hook:

Ginny is not having an easy time in middle school—in fact, just about everything seems to be going wrong for her. The story of her mishaps is told trough her stuff—receipts, to-do lists, horoscopes, IMs, notes from her Mom and brothers, newspaper articles, report cards, notes from friends and teachers, and more. With a light, humorous tone, this quick read fills in all the blanks of one true-to-life, recognizable seventh grader's school year.

Three words or phrases that best describe this book are:
• Engrossing pace
• Bittersweet tone
• Familiar/realistic characters
Note: Unique format (no paragraphs or chapters)

Name: O. Nesi

GET HOOKED ON READING!!

Title: *The Miraculous Journey of Edward Tulane*

Author: Kate DiCamillo

Genre: Fantasy

Here's the Hook:

Edward Tulane is a beautiful china rabbit doll. He is totally adored by his owner (a young girl named Abilene). Edward thinks very highly of himself and carelessly takes Abilene's love for granted. In fact, he is bored by it (just as he is bored by many of the advantages he has). When he is taken on a trip with Abilene's family and ends up lost, a new world slowly opens to him. Through joyous times and painful ones, Edward learns about love and its significance.

Three words or phrases that best describe this book are:
• Calm/gentle pace
• Heartwarming/poetic tone
• Deeply moving story line

Name: O. Nesi

GET HOOKED ON READING!!

Title: *The Misfits*

Author: James Howe

Genre: Realistic Fiction

Here's the Hook:

Have you ever been called a hurtful name? Join the Gang of Five (which actually turns out to be four kids) as they battle name calling in their middle school. Skeezie, Addie, Joe, and Bobby are each unique but completely united in their determination to put an end to the hurtful insults kids casually aim at them and each other. In this inspirational novel, four lifelike and well-developed characters create a series of events and take on the entire population of their school.

Three words or phrases that best describe this book are:
• Unhurried pace
• Issue-oriented story line
• Familiar/recognizable characters

Name: O. Nesi

GET HOOKED ON READING!!

Title: *The Missing Girl*

Author: Norma Fox Mazer

Genre: Realistic Fiction

Here's the Hook:

The individual personalities of five sisters ranging in age from eleven to seventeen are fully developed in this novel told from all five of their alternating points of view. Added to their chorus is the voice of a convicted child molester that secretly watches them and eventually entraps one of the girls. Both his voice and his lurking overpower the tone of the book, leaving the reader truly terrified and in a near-constant state of tension.

Three words or phrases that best describe this book are:
• Engrossing pace
• Suspenseful/tense tone
• Creepy/disturbing story line

Name: O. Nesi

From *Getting Beyond "Interesting": Teaching Students the Vocabulary of Appeal to Discuss Their Reading* by Olga M. Nesi. Santa Barbara, CA: Libraries Unlimited. Copyright © 2012.

GET HOOKED ON READING!!

Title: *The Mysterious Benedict Society*

Author: Trenton Lee Stewart

Genre: Mystery

Here's the Hook:

Recruited for a most special and secretive mission, Reynie, Sticky, Constance, and Kate form the Mysterious Benedict Society. Near-constant suspense is created by riddles, puzzles, and a gradually unfolding mystery. A carefully crafted plot advances deliberately with just the right amount of action, and plot twists to keep readers engaged in the story line. What appears to be a resolved ending gives way to a cliff-hanger: The Mysterious Benedict Society is nowhere near done solving mysteries.

Three words or phrases that best describe this book are:
• Deliberate pace
• Suspenseful tone
• Well-developed characters

Name: O. Nesi

GET HOOKED ON READING!!

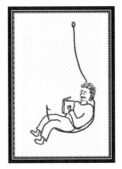

Title: *No Choirboy: Murder, Violence, and Teenagers on Death Row*

Author: Susan Kuklin

Genre: Nonfiction/Journalism

Here's the Hook:

Kevin was sixteen years old when he murdered a person. Mark was just fourteen, and Nanon and Napoleon were seventeen when they committed murders. In 2002 (after spending eight years on Death Row), Napoleon was put to death. His last words were: "No one wins tonight. No one gets closure. No one walks away victorious." In 2005, the Supreme Court ruled that if someone committed a murder and was less than eighteen years of age, he or she could no longer be sentenced to death. Kevin, Mark, and Nanon's sentences were changed to life without parole. Mary and Paul's brother William was in high school when he was murdered. No one in William's family wants his killer to be executed. Who is right? Who is wrong? And what is it like to know at sixteen, fourteen, and seventeen that you will live your entire life in prison?

Three words or phrases that best describe this book are:
• Dark/sad/hopeless tone
• Heartbreaking story lines
• Extremely thought provoking

Name: O. Nesi

GET HOOKED ON READING!!	**GET HOOKED ON READING!!**

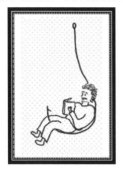

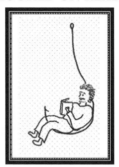

Title: *Pastworld*

Author: Ian Beck

Genre: Mystery

Here's the Hook:

This story is part science fiction, part historical fiction, and part mystery. In the year 2050, when citizens tire of living in the present, they can travel to Pastworld to get a true feel for the past. Designed to be a type of theme park, Pastworld completely recreates Victorian London for visitors so that they can experience what living in London in the 1800s was really like. Complete with its own serial killer (the Phantom), a visit to Pastworld turns into a nightmare for Caleb when he is accused of committing a murder. In this story, history comes alive, and an increasingly suspenseful story line builds tension until an unexpected ending reveals the truth about Pastworld and its creators.

Three words or phrases that best describe this book are:
• A deliberate pace gives way to a compelling one as the plot unfolds.
• Dark tone
• The story line has a couple of plot twists

Name: O. Nesi

Title: *Picture the Dead*

Author: Adele Griffin and Lisa Brown

Genre: Historical Fiction/Mystery/Ghost Story/Romance

Here's the Hook:

Part mystery/ghost story, part historical fiction romance, Jennie's story unfolds during the American Civil War. Both her parents and her brother Toby are dead. But when her fiancé Will dies in the war, the true haunting begins. Illustrated throughout, this is the story of Will reaching from beyond the grave to help Jennie discover the truth about how he died. This mildly spine-tingling and romantic tale is full of historical details and moments of ghostly creepiness.

Three words or phrases that best describe this book are:
• Deliberate pace
• Spooky tone alternates with a romantic tone
• Dramatic characters

Name: O. Nesi

GET HOOKED ON READING!!

Title: *Pieces of Georgia*

Author: Jen Bryant

Genre: Realistic Fiction

Here's the Hook:

Seventh grade is bad enough for most kids. For Georgia, it's even worse. Her mom died when she was in the second grade and she misses her terribly. Her dad cannot come to terms with the death, and they are poor. To ease some of the pain she is feeling, Georgia writes to her mom in a journal, sharing her secrets, worries, and even joys and triumphs

Three words or phrases that best describe this book are:
• Unhurried pace
• Quiet/gentle tone
• Character-driven/emotional story line

Name: O. Nesi

GET HOOKED ON READING!!

Title: *Poison*

Author: Chris Wooding

Genre: Fantasy

Here's the Hook:

Poison's sister Azalea has been abducted by phaeries. A blank-eyed changeling has been left in her place. Not one to ever pass up a challenge, Poison decides to travel to the Realm of the Phaeries to demand that the all-powerful Phaerie Lord return Azalea. Courageous and determined to the point of folly, Poison confronts and overcomes one darkly magical and terrifying obstacle after another in her journey to take back her sister.

Three words or phrases that best describe this book are:
• Fast pace
• Fantastical/spooky tone
• Twisty story line

Name: O. Nesi

GET HOOKED ON READING!!

Title: *The Rag and Bone Shop*

Author: Robert Cormier

Genre: Mystery/Realistic Fiction

Here's the Hook:

A seven-year-old girl is found murdered in a small New England town. An expert interrogator is brought in to question twelve-year-old Jason, who thinks he will be helping to solve the crime by agreeing to be interrogated. In fact, he is being coerced and manipulated into confessing he committed the murder. Inescapably dark, psychological, and tense, this disturbing novel is a play-by-play recounting of an expert questioner's techniques as he tries to break Jason down.

Three words or phrases that best describe this book are:
• Deliberate pace
• Nightmare tone
• Character-centered story line
Note: This novel is completely driven by the tension of the interrogation. There is very little action in it, yet the reader reads on, desperate to know the final outcome.

Name: O. Nesi

GET HOOKED ON READING!!

Title: *Remembering Raquel*

Author: Vivian Vande Velde

Genre: Realistic Fiction

Here's the Hook:

How did fourteen-year-old Raquel Falcone die? Was she accidentally or intentionally pushed in front of an oncoming car? Did she lose her footing and fall down under it? Or did she step in front of it on purpose? Told from the points of view of the people in her life, this quick read is full of small plot shifts and surprising plot twists, each packing a major emotional punch.

Three words or phrases that best describe this book are:
• Engrossing pace
• Psychological tone
• Multiple points of view characterization

Name: O. Nesi

From *Getting Beyond "Interesting": Teaching Students the Vocabulary of Appeal to Discuss Their Reading* by Olga M. Nesi. Santa Barbara, CA: Libraries Unlimited. Copyright © 2012.

GET HOOKED ON READING!!	**GET HOOKED ON READING!!**

Title: *Revolver*

Author: Marcus Sedgwick

Genre: Thriller/Mystery/Historical Fiction

Here's the Hook:

Set in Alaska during the gold rush in the late 1800s, this mystery is gripping and literally chilling. Sig's father Einar is dead, and Sig knows nothing of the debt a threatening stranger claims to be owed by Einar. A tense and suspenseful tone alternates with deep foreboding and menace. The dark and frigid Alaska winter provides a stark and grim background to this relentlessly taut story. A Colt revolver adds to the sense of unpredictability. A hairpin plot twist is both completely unexpected and deeply satisfying.

Three words or phrases that best describe this book are:
• Compelling pace
• Foreboding and menacing tone
• Multiple plot lines

Name: O. Nesi

Title: *Right Behind You*

Author: Gail Giles

Genre: Realistic Fiction/Problem Novel

Here's the Hook:

How destructive can anger be? Destructive enough to land nine-year-old Kip in a psychiatric ward for criminally violent youth after he kills a seven-year-old neighbor by setting him on fire. How long can anger that destructive last? Well into Kip's fourteenth year of life, when he is finally released from the facility and has to find a way to learn to control it or risk repeatedly tearing his family apart. In this tense, character-driven, and emotionally charged novel, readers are living in Kip's skin, unable to escape his anger and fear until he finds a way to escape them himself.

Three words or phrases that best describe this book are:
• Compelling pace
• Hard-edged/edgy tone and frame
• Character-driven plot

Name: O. Nesi

GET HOOKED ON READING!!	**GET HOOKED ON READING!!**

<table>
<tr>
<td>

Title: *Rikers High*

Author: Paul Volponi

Genre: Realistic Fiction/Problem Novel

Here's the Hook:

Realistic and gritty, this is Martin's story. On the outside, his life might not have been perfect, but on Rikers Island, it is truly frightening. Readers live inside Martin as he figures out how to live in jail and tries desperately not to lose himself completely in the ugliness of the place. Totally true to life and psychologically dark, *Rikers High* is as real as any story about young people in jail can get. Details about daily life and hardships are found throughout the book. This is not an easy story to read . . . raw and tough.

Three words or phrases that best describe this book are:
• Deliberate pace—you will "feel" the days as Martin does.
• Bleak, psychological, and heavy tone
• Character-centered story line
Note: This is an eighth-grade book

Name: O. Nesi

</td>
<td>

Title: *Robot Dreams*

Author: Sara Varon

Genre: Wordless Graphic Novel

Here's the Hook:

If you've ever made and then later lost a friend due to circumstances completely out of your control, this story is for you. Dog and Robot are friends. A Labor Day incident at the beach causes their friendship to come completely apart. Packed with a wide variety of immediately recognizable human emotions and difficulties, this quick read hops from one surprise to another and leaves you thinking about the subject of friendship long after the story is done.

Three words or phrases that best describe this book are:
• Pace can be either fast or leisurely, depending on how much time you devote to studying the pictures.
• Bittersweet tone
• Character-centered story line

Name: O. Nesi

</td>
</tr>
</table>

GET HOOKED ON READING!!	**GET HOOKED ON READING!!**

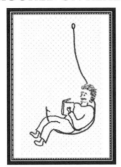

Title: *Ruined—A Ghost Story*

Author: Paula Morris

Genre: Ghost Story

Here's the Hook:

A wealthy New Orleans family . . . a 200-year-old curse . . . the ghost of a young murdered girl haunting the family and the nearby cemetery . . . all these elements, added to a foreboding and suspenseful tone, keep the reader wondering if the curse will ever be lifted from the Bowman family daughters and if the murdered girl's ghost will ever be released from earth. What will it take to let the dead rest?

Three words or phrases that best describe this book are:
• Deliberate pace
• Suspenseful tone
• Character-centered story line
Note: This is a mild ghost story—not too scary. If you prefer extremely frightening books, pass on this one. If, on the other hand, you like mildly tingly ghost tales, this one is perfect.

Name: O. Nesi

Title: *The Rules of Survival*

Author: Nancy Werlin

Genre: Realistic Fiction

Here's the Hook:

Matt is thirteen, Callie is eleven, and Emmy is five. All three of their lives are a rollercoaster ride of physical and emotional abuse at the hands of their mother, Nikki. Struggling to survive, they develop coping strategies to deal with their mother's unpredictable personality, drug use, and episodes of hair-raising violence.

Three words or phrases that best describe this book are:
• Claustrophobic tone
• Emotionally draining story line
• Well-developed/realistic characters

Name: O. Nesi

GET HOOKED ON READING!!

Title: *The Savage*

Author: David Almond

Illustrator: Dave McKean

Genre: Magical Realism

Here's the Hook:

Blue Baker's life is mostly sad, especially since his father died. His one joy is writing stories. His story about the Savage is brutal and bloody and adventurous, and he enjoys having the beast torment the town bully. Then, in a startling plot twist, the Savage mysteriously and surprisingly comes to life.

Does the Savage truly exist, or is he simply the product of Blue's overactive imagination?

Three words or phrases that best describe this book are:
• Fast pace
• Creepy, dark tone
• Mystical story line

Name: O. Nesi

GET HOOKED ON READING!!

Title: *Saving Zoe*

Author: Alyson Noel

Genre: Realistic Fiction

Here's the Hook:

On top of having to deal with being new to the eighth grade, Echo is trying desperately to come to terms with the brutal murder of her eighteen-year-old sister Zoe and her town's constant gossip about her sister and the crime. By reading Zoe's journal, Echo hopes to find peace, as well as some explanation as to what led Zoe to the situation that resulted in her murder. Above all else, however, Echo wants to save the memory of Zoe from being ruined by others.

Three words or phrases that best describe this book are:
• Engrossing pace
• Emotional tone
• Lifelike characters

Name: O. Nesi

GET HOOKED ON READING!!

Title: *Schooled*

Author: Gordon Korman

Genre: Humorous Realistic Fiction

Here's the Hook:

His grandmother's name is Rain. His name is Capricorn. She has raised him as a hippie on Garland Farms for his entire life. He has known no one but her for all of his thirteen years. He knows nothing of the outside world. Then one day, she falls out of a tree, breaks her hip, and has to be taken to the hospital. Capricorn is brought into town, put into foster care, and forced to go to a regular school. That's when the comical misadventures, misunderstandings, and surprises begin. How does a thirteen-year-old genuine hippie survive in a modern-day middle school?

Three words or phrases that best describe this book are:
• Humorous tone
• Inspirational story line
• Multiple points of view in characterization

Name: O. Nesi

GET HOOKED ON READING!!

Title: *The Schwa Was Here*

Author: Neal Schusterman

Genre: Humorous Realistic Fiction

Here's the Hook:

What does it feel like to be practically invisible to others? Is it an advantage, or does it hurt to know that no one ever notices your presence? Anthony Bonano and his friends cannot believe they never noticed Calvin Schwa before. They're all in the same class at school, but "the Schwa," for some mysterious reason, is nearly invisible to others. People don't realize he is standing right next to them until he speaks and they nearly jump out of their skins. The kid just blends into the background—no matter where he is. By turns funny and thought-provoking, this novel reveals both what is good and what is definitely bad about the Schwa's invisibility effect.

Three words or phrases that best describe this book are:
• Humorous tone
• Poignant story line
• Quirky secondary characters

Name: O. Nesi

GET HOOKED ON READING!!

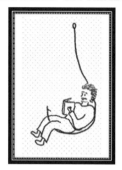

Title: *Secret Saturdays*

Author: Torrey Maldonado

Genre: Urban Realistic Fiction/Problem Novel

Here's the Hook:

Growing up in the Red Hook Projects is not easy for Justin, Sean, Vanessa, and Kyle, and school is a minefield of "dis or be dissed." Friendships and family are the main supports in the lives of these sixth graders. What happens when Justin suspects Sean of lying to him and their group of friends? What makes Sean unable to share what he is feeling with his closest friends, and how will they help him get his life back on track if they are kept in the dark about Sean's Secret Saturdays?

Three words or phrases that best describe this book are:
• Easy pace
• Urban tone
• Issue oriented story line

Name: O. Nesi

GET HOOKED ON READING!!

Title: *The Seer of Shadows*

Author: Avi

Genre: Historical Fiction/Ghost Story

Here's the Hook:

The year is 1872, and fourteen-year-old Horace Carpentine is apprenticed to a photographer in New York City. Little does he know that he will soon discover a special talent he has for creating living ghosts through the process of taking and developing photographs. Join him on his spine-tingling, hair-raising adventures as he gives life once again to a dead, abused little girl named Eleanora. In this gripping tale of ghostly vengeance, the pages keep turning—nearly outside of your own power.

Three words or phrases that best describe this book are:
• Steady pace
• Spooky/foreboding/suspenseful tone
• Layered story line

Name: O. Nesi

GET HOOKED ON READING!!

Title: *Shark Girl*

Author: Kelly Bingham

Genre: Realistic Fiction

Here's the Hook:

If only fifteen-year-old Jane hadn't gone to the beach that day . . . if only she had left her house five minutes later . . . if only she hadn't gone in the water—she might not have lost her right arm to a shark attack, and she might still want to be an artist someday. But she did go to the beach and she didn't leave five minutes earlier and she did go in the water—so her arm is gone and she will never be the same . . . but maybe, just maybe, she will be a better person than she was before.

Three words or phrases that best describe this book are:
• Engrossing pace
• Emotional tone
• Character-driven story line

Name: O. Nesi

GET HOOKED ON READING!!

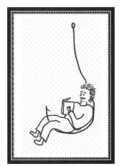

Title: *Shifty*

Author: Lynn E. Hazen

Genre: Realistic Fiction/Problem Novel

Here's the Hook:

Soli gets the nickname Shifty while living in a group home for boys because he's really good at getting into trouble and then figuring out how to wiggle out of it. Now he's in foster care with Martha and would like to stop being moved around so much. If he wants to stay, he will have to figure out how to stay out of trouble in the first place. This story alternates between suspenseful, action-driven scenes and gentle, family-centered moments. The reader lives inside Shifty and learns how he thinks and feels about his life, the situations he gets himself into, and what he will have to do to set and keep things straight.

Three words or phrases that best describe this book are:
• Easy pace
• Bittersweet tone
• Well-developed characters

Name: O. Nesi

GET HOOKED ON READING!!

Title: *Slam*

Author: Nick Hornby

Genre: Humorous Realistic Fiction

Here's the Hook:

Fifteen-year-old skateboarding-obsessed boy (Sam) meets beautiful fifteen-year-old girl (Alicia). Boy dates girl. Boy and girl make a mistake and become parents. Told from Sam's point of view and in part through his imaginary chats with Tony Hawk, this funny, moving, and dead-on story relays precisely what it must feel like to be a fifteen-year-old boy and find out you are soon going to be a father.

Note: This story is set in London, England.

Three words or phrases that best describe this book are:
• Bittersweet tone
• Completely character-driven story line
• Extremely real/lifelike characters

Name: O. Nesi

GET HOOKED ON READING!!

Title: *Slob*

Author: Ellen Potter

Genre: Realistic Fiction

Here's the Hook:

Twelve-year-old Owen Birnbaum is definitely fatter than you. He's probably also much smarter than you. In fact, he is just one point short of being an official genius, so you can imagine how much he is tortured and bullied at school. Why does his sister want to be called Jeremy? Why is the fiercest-looking kid in the school apparently on a mission to ruin him? Where are the answers to all the questions he has about feeling small and lost inside himself? Perhaps he can create a machine that will tell him everything he wants to know.

By turns funny and sad, this is a story that takes readers deep into the heart of a bright, gentle, somewhat confused, genuinely real, and likeable character.

Three words or phrases that best describe this book are:
• Deliberate pace
• Bittersweet tone
• Character-centered story line

Name: O. Nesi

GET HOOKED ON READING!!

Title: *Smile*

Author: Raina Telgemeier

Genre: Graphic Novel

Here's the Hook:

Based in part on the author's personal experiences, *Smile* is a light and humorous look at dental catastrophe and trauma. While running, sixth grader Raina trips, falls, and permanently damages her front teeth. The next four years of her life are all about visits to dentists as they try a number of techniques to repair her smile. Along the way, Raina experiences true-to-life embarrassments and friendship disappointments. With realistic characters and a completely engrossing story line, *Smile* delivers a gutsy, smart, and courageous character.

Three words or phrases that best describe this book are:
• Engaging tone
• Character-centered story line
• Realistic characters

Name: O. Nesi

GET HOOKED ON READING!!

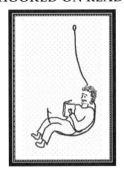

Title: *Stuck in Neutral*

Author: Terry Trueman

Genre: Realistic Fiction

Here's the Hook:

Completely trapped in his own body, fourteen-year-old Shawn McDaniel is incredibly smart but totally paralyzed. He cannot even speak. Cerebral palsy has imprisoned him. He has been this way as long as he can remember, and now he suspects his father is planning to kill him to "put him out of his misery." If you dare, enter the "cage" that is Shawn's body and live with his thoughts and feelings as he struggles to come to terms with his father's plan.

Three words or phrases that best describe this book are:
• Compelling pace
• Psychological/claustrophobic tone
• Open-ended story line

Name: O. Nesi

GET HOOKED ON READING!!	**GET HOOKED ON READING!!**
	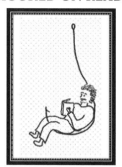

Title: *The True Meaning of Smekday*

Author: Adam Rex

Genre: Science Fiction/Humor

Here's the Hook:

Gratuity Tucci is separated from her mom when the Boov (an alien species) invade and take over the earth. She befriends a Boov named J. Lo, and together they go off in search of her mother. Several days into their adventure and crisis-filled journey to Arizona (where all humans have been relocated), the Gorg invade earth. Additional chaos ensues.

Three words or phrases that best describe this book are:
• Engrossing pace
• Humorous tone
• Unpredictable story line

Name: O. Nesi

Title: *Twisted*

Author: Laurie Halse Anderson

Genre: Realistic Fiction

Here's the Hook:

Tyler Miller is invisible to everyone but his angry, miserable father and an assortment of bullies at school until a graffiti stunt lands him in hard labor for the summer and gains him both a criminal reputation and the attention of girls. When his life starts to spiral out of control, Tyler realizes he has difficult and painful choices to make. He will either transform himself or remain trapped in others' perceptions of him.

Three words or phrases that best describe this book are:
• Tense/taut tone
• Gripping story line
• Realistic characters

Name: O. Nesi

GET HOOKED ON READING!!

Title: *Uncle Montague's Tales of Terror*

Author: Chris Priestley

Genre: Fantasy/Ghost Stories

Here's the Hook:

Edgar's secretive and spooky Uncle Montague lives in a creepy, unheated house with no electricity in the middle of a dark, foggy forest. Whenever he can, Edgar visits his uncle and sits by the fire with him, listening to one ghostly, chilling tale after another. The flames from the fire cast eerily dancing shadows into the dark corners of the parlor, and everywhere Edgar looks, his eyes land on an assortment of odd objects, each with a deliciously spine-tingling story all its own. Where do all these stories come from, and what, exactly, is Uncle Montague's secret?

Three words or phrases that best describe this book are:
• Creepy/spooky tone
• Episodic story line (each story stands on its own)
• Eccentric/quirky characters

Name: O. Nesi

GET HOOKED ON READING!!

Title: *Unwind*

Author: Neal Schusterman

Genre: Science Fiction

Here's the Hook:

Unwinding: a procedure in which the bodies of unwanted kids between the ages of thirteen and eighteen are taken apart piece by piece and harvested for use by others.

In a world gone absolutely mad, Connor, Lev, and Risa are running for their lives—desperate to escape being unwound. By turns frantic, angry, fearful, and hopeless, the teens' fight for their lives is full of white-knuckled tension, page-turning suspense, and dizzying action.

Three words or phrases that best describe this book are:
• Fast pace
• Disturbing/edgy tone
• Action-packed story line

Name: O. Nesi

GET HOOKED ON READING!!

Title: *Voss—How I Come to America and Am Hero, Mostly*

Author: David Ives

Genre: Humorous Realistic (?) Fiction

Here's the Hook:

Vospop Vszlzwczdztwczky is a fifteen-year-old Slobovian immigrant writing letters to his friend Meero back home, telling him all about his misadventures in America. With a light, humorous tone, plenty of word play, and several hilarious misunderstandings caused by limited English, this novel reveals Voss to be a gentle, intelligent, and altogether completely likable character.

Three words or phrases that best describe this book are:
• Light, humorous tone
• Quirky, likable main character
• Easy pace and resolved ending

Name: O. Nesi

GET HOOKED ON READING!!

Title: *We Were Here*

Author: Matt De La Pena

Genre: Realistic Fiction/Problem Novel

Here's the Hook:

Miguel is locked tightly inside himself. No one can know about the crime he committed that got him sent to a group home for a year. He cannot even bear to think of it. Intelligent, introspective, and desperately ashamed of what he did, Miguel withdraws completely and feigns total indifference. In this gritty first-person narrative (written in journal form), Miguel gradually reveals to readers his innermost secrets, fears, and thoughts and, in the end, matures most when he learns to forgive himself.

Three words or phrases that best describe this book are:
• Deliberate pace
• Bleak, psychological, and heavy tone
• Character-centered story line

Name: O. Nesi

GET HOOKED ON READING!!

Title: *The Well*

Author: A. J. Whitten

Genre: Horror/Thriller

Here's the Hook:

In this spine-tingling and truly creepy novel, fifteen-year-old Cooper suspects his mother is trying to kill him. That's about as bad as things can get—until he finds himself at the bottom of a well with a creature lurking in the darkness, trying to devour him and drink his blood. Cooper escapes on a number of occasions but continues to be stalked by the beast as the mystery of his stepfather's vineyard is gradually revealed. Suspense builds to a fever pitch as Cooper struggles to figure out a way to keep himself safe and alive.

Three words or phrases that best describe this book are:
• Compelling pace
• Creepy/nightmare tone
• Dramatic characters

Name: O. Nesi

GET HOOKED ON READING!!

Title: *What Happened to Cass McBride?*

Author: Gail Giles

Genre: Mystery

Here's the Hook:

Here's what happened to Cass McBride: Kyle Kirby will not let her get away with causing his brother's suicide.

In this suspenseful, taut, and tension-filled thriller, alternating voices tell the story of Kyle's revenge against Cass—beautiful Cass, popular Cass, manipulative Cass—Cass who is now buried alive and completely at Kyle's mercy for air . . . for water . . . for her life. Regardless of whether the detectives find her in her living tomb, she will suffer for rejecting David.

Three words or phrases that best describe this book are:
• Compelling pace
• Dark tone
• Multiple points of view in characterization

Name: O. Nesi

GET HOOKED ON READING!!

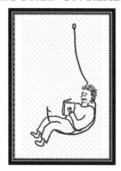

Title: *Wintergirls*

Author: Laurie Halse Anderson

Genre: Realistic Fiction/Problem Novel

Here's the Hook:

Wintergirls are girls who want to be the thinnest girls. Wintergirls are anorexic and bulimic. Sometimes, Wintergirls die.

Lia and Cassie are best friends and Wintergirls together . . . until Cassie starves herself to death, leaving Lia stranded in a landscape of pain, fear, and anger. Told in the first person from Lia's point of view, this deeply painful and dark book literally forces readers to live in Lia's tormented mind as she gradually descends into total despair. Inescapably heartbreaking and terrifying, *Wintergirls* will leave you gasping for air.

Three words or phrases that best describe this book are:
• Compelling pace
• Psychological tone
• Realistic characters

Name: O. Nesi

GET HOOKED ON READING!!

Title: *You*

Author: Charles Benoit

Genre: Realistic Fiction/Problem Novel

Here's the Hook:

A driving pace, tension, and a near-constant sense of foreboding dominate this novel. From the first page to the very last, the reader is literally trapped in the story—hoping the worst won't happen but knowing that it must.

Kyle Chase is not a bad kid—just angry, depressed, lost, and madly in love with Ashley Bianchi. Until his path crosses that of Zack McDade, he's just cruising along in the underachiever lane—mostly miserable, but certainly not in any danger until things begin to quickly spiral out of control. After all, a sociopath like Zack cannot be happy unless he is in total control and destroying the people around him.

Three words or phrases that best describe this book are:
• Compelling pace
• Foreboding tone
• Character-centered story line

Name: O. Nesi

Appendix B-8

Book Hooks for *Winston the Book Wolf* by Marni McGee and Ian Beck (London: Bloomsbury Children's Books, 2006)

Book Hooks

Have you devoured any books lately? Winston's insatiable appetite for a good book has gotten him into serious trouble. In fact, he is banned from the library. Eat words with your eyes, Rosie teaches him. With a unique twist on familiar yet quirky characters, this charming fractured fairy tale is lively, humorous, and engaging. <div align="right">R. Deutsch, M. Dennehy, C. Hagarty, E. Naylor Gutierrez, O. Nesi, and J. Schaffner</div>
When books are your favorite food, the library becomes your favorite place. In this lively and upbeat tale, quirky Winston passes up the cheeseburgers in favor of words, getting himself banned from the library for nibbling on books. After Winston gobbles up the sign "No wolves Allowed," will he ever be allowed in the library again? <div align="right">T. Tartaglione</div>
Winston loves books. He loves them so much he wants to eat them up. But the librarian won't let this wily wolf through the door. Find out how Winston schemes and sneaks into the library (perhaps with a grandmother's dress?). What would *you* do to find a book you love? <div align="right">L. Ellis</div>
No wolves allowed...in the library. But Winston the Wolf hungers for words. He is on the outside looking in. Read this book to find out how he enters the world of words. With vivid characters and surprising plot twists, you too will devour the words and savor the story of Winston the Wolf. <div align="right">E. Cummings and B. Shufelt</div>
The library door says "No Wolves Allowed," but Winston the Book Wolf eats the sign and goes in anyway. How will he find his way back into the library after this horrible behavior and still get a steady diet of tasty words? You'll love this lively, funny, fractured fairy tale...or I'll eat my words! <div align="right">M. Ahart</div>

From: Getting Beyond Interesting. . .

Appendix B-9

What Appeals to You?

Pace	Tone
breakneck	bittersweet
compelling	bleak
deliberate	contemporary
densely written	creepy
easy	dark
engrossing	detailed setting
fast	edgy
leisurely	engaging
measured	exotic
relaxed	foreboding
stately	gritty
unhurried	hard edged
	heartwarming
	humorous
	lush
	magical
	melodramatic
	menacing
	mystical
	nightmare
	political
	psychological
	romantic
	spooky
	stark
	suspenseful
	timeless
	upbeat
	urban

Story Line	Characters or Characterization
action oriented	detailed
character centered	distant
complex	dramatic
domestic	eccentric
episodic	evocative
fact filled	faithful
family centered	familiar
gentle	intriguing secondary characters
inspirational	introspective
issue oriented	lifelike
layered	multiple points of view
multiple plotlines	quirky
mystical	realistic
mythic	recognizable
open ended	series characters

plot centered plot twists resolved ending rich and famous thought provoking tragic violent	vivid well developed well drawn

Appendix B-10
Appeal Terms Glossary

action oriented: Used to describe the story line of a book.

If the story line of a book is action oriented, this usually means the plot is driven by action. The story unfolds through a series of events that involve the characters. The action of the story is external and the reader gets to know the characters mainly by their reactions to the action in the story. These books tend to feel action packed.

bittersweet: Used to describe the tone of a book.

A book with a bittersweet tone makes readers feel both sad and joyful as they read it.

bleak: Used to describe the tone of a book.

If a book has a bleak tone, it is joyless and creates a feeling of heaviness in the reader.

breakneck: Used to describe the pace of a book.

If the pace of a book is breakneck, the reader is moved through the story line extremely fast.

character centered: Used to describe the story line of a book.

If the story line of a book is character centered, this usually means the plot is driven by the actions and thoughts of the characters. The action of the story is internal and the story itself is told mainly through the characters' thoughts, feelings, and actions. These books tend to have an emotional and/or psychological feel to them.

characters or characterization: Describes the various types of characters, how the author creates them, and the ways in which readers respond to them.

compelling: Used to describe the pace of a book.

If the pace of a book is compelling, it forces you to keep reading, usually because you want to know what will happen next.

complex: Used to describe the story line of a book.

A story line that is complex unfolds in a number of ways at once. It may be both action oriented and character centered, external and internal at once.

contemporary: Used to describe the tone of a book.

If a book has a contemporary tone, the reader will feel as though the story could take place in the present time.

creepy: Used to describe the tone of a book.

If a book has a creepy tone, the reader will feel fearful and uncomfortable.

dark: Used to describe the tone of a book.

If a book has a dark tone, it may also feel bleak. The darkness may be experienced by the reader as a heaviness of subject matter. Books with a darkly humorous tone "lighten" the darkness somewhat.

deliberate: Used to describe the pace of a book.

If the pace of a book is deliberate, it is unhurried on purpose. The author made a conscious decision to tell the story in a controlled way. Usually, this adds to the tension created in stories.

densely written: Used to describe the pace of a book.

Books that have a dense pace are often difficult to move through quickly. These books may be overly descriptive or the language employed by the author may be overly florid. In any event, because they require careful and thoughtful reading, the pace at which the story appears to be moving slows down.

detailed: Used to describe the characters or characterization of a book.

Characters are detailed if the reader is given a fair amount of descriptive information about them. This description will help the reader to "see" the character.

detailed setting: Used to describe the tone of a book.

The tone of a book is affected by how much setting detail the author creates. A good example might be historical fiction. Extra detail about the setting (specific to a time period in history) helps to create the tone of the story.

distant: Used to describe the characters in a book.

Distant characters seem unfamiliar, cold, unfeeling, removed, uncaring, and unfriendly. The reader may have a difficult time relating to or feeling empathy toward distant characters.

domestic: Used to describe the story line of a book.

If the story line of a book is domestic, this usually means the plot is driven by the actions and emotions within a family. The story unfolds through family situations and relationships.

dramatic: Used to describe the characters or characterization of a book.

Dramatic characters are highly emotional. Their responses to situations are often unpredictable and overblown. If all of a book's characterization is dramatic, then all its characters are highly emotional.

easy: Used to describe the pace of a book.

Easy pacing may make the experience of reading a book seem effortless. The story advances at a comfortable pace for the reader.

eccentric: Used to describe the characters in a book.

Eccentric characters are not ordinary. They think and behave in unusual and extraordinary ways.

edgy: Used to describe the tone of a book.

An edgy tone makes the reader feel tense and uncomfortable.

engaging: Used to describe the tone of a book.

A book with an engaging tone makes readers want to continue to concentrate on and commit to the story.

engrossing: Used to describe the pace of a book.

If the pace of a book is engrossing, it holds the reader's attention.

episodic: Used to describe the story line of a book.

If the story line of a book is episodic, this usually means each event that is part of the story can stand on its own as a separate whole. For example: Stories told from multiple points of view and in alternating voices may feel episodic since each person's story is complete on its own.

event oriented: Used to describe the story line of a book.

A story line that is event oriented unfolds around a particular event, be it personal (a family visit) or historical (the Chicago Fire).

evocative: Used to describe the characters or characterization of a book.

Evocative characters elicit emotional and empathetic responses from readers.

exotic: Used to describe the tone of a book.

An exotic tone is one that is highly unusual or unfamiliar to the reader.

fact filled: Used to describe the story line of a book.

Applies mostly to nonfiction but can also be used to describe story lines that include factual details about particular topics. Historical fiction novels may have story lines that are fact filled, as the author describes the setting of the novel using historical facts as a background to the story.

faithful: Used to describe the characters or characterization in a book.

Faithful characters or characterization are accurate and realistic.

familiar: Used to describe the characters or characterization in a book.

Familiar characters are recognizable to readers.

family centered: Used to describe the story line of a book.

If the story line of a book is family centered, this usually means the plot is driven by family relationships and events. Family-centered and domestic story lines can be similar.

fast: Used to describe the pace of a book.

If the pace of a book is fast, the reader is moved along through the story rapidly.

foreboding: Used to describe the tone of a book.

A book with a foreboding tone creates in readers the feeling that something bad is going happen.

gentle: Used to describe the story line of a book.

If the story line of a book is gentle, this usually means the plot moves along evenly and quietly. There are no dramatic or jarring events in the plot.

gritty: Used to describe the tone of a book.

The tone of a book is gritty if the characters in the story show resolve and strength in the face of great challenges and difficulties.

hard edged: Used to describe the tone of a book.

If a book's tone is hard edged, it is tough and direct.

heartwarming: Used to describe the tone of a book.

A heartwarming tone is cheering to one's emotions.

heavy: Used to describe the tone of a book.

A heavy tone is ponderous and more than likely evokes sadness and desperation.

hopeful: Used to describe the tone of a book.

If the tone of a book is hopeful, the reader expects the story's outcome to be positive.

humorous: Used to describe the tone of a book.

If the tone of a book is humorous, it is funny.

inspirational: Used to describe the story line of a book.

If the story line of a book is inspirational, the events of the plot act on or move the reader's emotions. The book may feel uplifting and might cause the reader to view a typically difficult situation in a new and more positive way.

internal: Used to describe books that are largely centered on the thoughts, emotions, and reactions of characters.

Books with an internal feel tend not to be action driven, as they are primarily about a character's perceptions and feelings and are told largely through the character's voice.

intriguing secondary characters: Used to describe the characters or characterization in a novel.

Secondary characters are characters that are not central to the story but important nonetheless. Intriguing secondary characters arouse the interest of the reader, are equally well developed as primary ones, and contribute to the story and its tone and feel.

introspective: Used to describe the characters in a book.

Characters that are introspective examine their own thoughts or feelings. The reader reacts to this by feeling as though they are inside the heads or hearts of the characters.

issue oriented: Used to describe the story line of a book.

If the story line of a book is issue oriented, the story is centered on a specific issue (e.g., bullying, anorexia, global warming, racism, etc.), and the events of the plot bring increased awareness about the issue.

layered: Used to describe the story line of a book.

A story line is layered if a variety of events, points of view, or issues are introduced one at a time and build on each other. Layered story lines tend to be complex.

leisurely: Used to describe the pace of a book.

If the pace of a book is leisurely, it is calm.

Lifelike: Used to describe the characters or characterization in a book.

Characters that are lifelike strike the reader as being real.

Lively: Used to describe the pace of a book.

A pace that is lively is brisk.

lush: Used to describe the tone of a book.

The tone of a book is lush if it creates the feeling of richness and luxuriousness. This is often achieved through the extensive description of setting, but it may also refer to the richness of the language itself.

magical: Used to describe the tone of a book.

Often in books with a magical tone, the seemingly impossible and highly improbable occur. Sometimes a magical tone is created by the subtle conveyance of a deep understanding and appreciation of a particular issue or concept (i.e., overcoming adversity or the glory of nature).

measured: Used to describe the pace of a book.

If the pace of a book is measured, it is even throughout. A measured pace is similar to a deliberate pace. In both cases, the author is careful about how (s)he wants to move readers through the book.

melodramatic: Used to describe the tone of a book.

A melodramatic tone makes the reader feel extreme emotions.

menacing: Used to describe the tone of a book.

In books with a menacing tone, the author conveys the threatening and imminent sense of danger in which characters find themselves.

multiple plot lines: Used to describe the story line of a book.

The story line of a book can be described as having multiple plot lines if several stories appear to be unfolding at once.

multiple points of view: Used to describe the characterization in a book.

Multiple points of view are used when a story is told from the points of view of several different characters. From this type of characterization, readers gain the individual perspectives of each of the characters.

mystical: Can be used to describe either the tone of a book or its story line.

A book with a mystical tone or story line feels otherworldly.

mythic: Used to describe the story line of a book.

If the story line of a book is mythic, this usually means the plot is driven by completely imaginary events.

nightmare: Used to describe the tone of a book.

A book with a nightmare tone may feel inescapable and may create a sense of dread in the reader.

open ended: Used to describe the story line of a book.

A book with an open-ended story line is one with an unresolved ending. The reader is left to imagine the ways in which the story might end.

pacing: Describes how quickly or slowly the author takes the reader through the story arc of the book.

plot centered: Used to describe the story line of a book.

A story line is plot centered if it is tightly organized around the events in the plot.

plot twists: Used to describe the story line of a book.

A story line that has plot twists takes the reader through a series of unpredictable events. Plot twists usually add to the suspense of a story because the reader cannot predict what will happen next and is often surprised by the twist.

political: Used to describe the tone of a book.

In books with a political tone, a particular agenda or stance may be conveyed.

psychological: Used to describe the tone of a book.

Books with a psychological tone take the reader into the minds of their characters.

quiet: Used to describe the tone of a book.

A quiet tone is subtle and may be paired with a gentle story line to create a calm atmosphere within which the story unfolds.

quirky: Used to describe the characters in a book.

A character that is quirky will display unusual or peculiar behaviors, mannerisms, and thought patterns.

realistic: Used to describe the characters or characterization in a book.

Realistic characters seem real to the reader. Authors who are good at creating realistic characters in novels may make readers feel that their characters actually exist somewhere in the world. Often, realistic characters are recognizable to readers. They may also seem familiar to the reader.

recognizable: Used to describe the characters in a book.

Recognizable characters are characters that seem familiar, realistic, and lifelike to readers.

relaxed: Used to describe the pace of a book.

If the pace of a book is relaxed, it is calm. A relaxed pace is similar to a leisurely pace and an unhurried pace. Note: Relaxed, leisurely, and unhurried stories are not necessarily boring.

resolved ending: Used to describe the story line of a book.

A story line with a resolved ending is one in which the conflict of the story is solved.

rich and famous: Used to describe the story line of a book.

If the story line of a book is "rich and famous," the events of the plot unfold in the worlds of the rich and famous and may contain frequent references to the accouterments of these worlds.

romantic: Used to describe the tone of a book.

In a story with a romantic tone, language is used to create a sentimental or idealistic mood. Moods created by romantic tones may vary greatly from each other and may be as different from each other as dreaminess and passion and extravagance and tenderness.

sad: Used to describe the tone of a book.

In a story with a sad tone, the language used by the author evokes melancholy.

series characters: Used to describe the characters in a book.

A series character is a character that appears in all the books in a particular series. Such a character is well known to readers of the series.

setting oriented: Used to describe the story line of a book.

A story line that is setting oriented is focused on the setting and relies on it to some extent to advance the plot. An example of this might be Tara, the plantation in Margaret Mitchell's novel *Gone With the Wind*.

spooky: Used to describe the tone of a book.

A story with a spooky tone is frightening but probably not horrifying.

stark: Used to describe the tone of a book.

A book with a stark tone evokes barrenness and desolation.

stately: Used to describe the pace of a book.

If the pace of a book is stately, its manner of advancing is kinglike. Kings do not run or rush. They move with dignity and purpose.

story line: The impact of the events of the plot on the feel of the book.

suspenseful: Used to describe the tone of a book.

A suspenseful tone creates tension and excitement as the reader wonders what will happen next.

thought provoking: Used to describe the story line of a book.

A book with a thought-provoking story line provides the reader with food for thought.

timeless: Used to describe the tone of a book.

A book with a timeless tone will make the reader feel that due to the universality of the events, the story could be taking place at any time.

tone: Describes how a reader feels while reading a book. The tone of a book can also be thought of as its feel or mood.

tragic: Used to describe the story line of a book.

If the story line of a book is tragic, the reader feels the conflict of the story is avoidable if not for the characters' mistakes and poor judgment.

unhurried: Used to describe the pace of a book.

If the pace of a book is unhurried, it is not fast. It is leisurely, relaxed, and easy.

upbeat: Used to describe the tone of a book.

A book with an upbeat tone creates feelings of optimism and cheerfulness in readers.

urban: Used to describe the tone of a book.

An urban tone is usually created in books that are set in cities.

violent: Used to describe the story line of a book.

If the story line of a book is violent, this usually means the plot is driven by violent events and/or action.

vivid: Used to describe the characters or characterization in a book.

Vivid characters are well developed and make a strong impression on readers.

well developed: Used to describe the characters or characterization in a book.

Characters are well developed when the author deliberately and carefully gives more and more details about them to the reader. At the end of having read a book with well-developed characters, readers may feel as though they truly and actually know them.

well drawn: Used to describe the characters or characterization in a book.

Well-drawn characters are characters for which the author has given much physical description. These are characters readers can actually see in their minds.

Bibliography

Avi. 2008. *The Seer of Shadows*. New York: HarperCollins Publishers.

Canton, Jeffrey. 2007. "Eye of the Crow: The Boy Sherlock Holmes: His First Case." Review of *The Eye of the Crow* by, by Shane Peacock. *Quill & Quire*, July 2007. http://quillandquire.com/books_young/review.cfm?review_id=5640.

Child, Lauren. 2005. *But Excuse Me That Is My Book*. New York: Dial Books for Young Readers.

Collins, Suzanne. 2009. *The Hunger Games*. New York: Scholastic.

Falconer, Ian. 2000. *Olivia*. New York: Atheneum Books for Young Readers.

Gaiman, Neil. 2004. *The Day I Swapped My Dad for Two Goldfish*. New York: Harper Collins Publishers.

The Girls Book Club. 2009. "Unwind by Neil Shusterman." *SyFy Imagine Greater Blog*, May 14. http://www.syfy.co.uk/blog/books/unwind-by-neil-shusterman.

Glantz, Shelley. 2008. "Unwind." Review of *Unwind*, by Neal Shusterman. Library Media Connection, Vol. 26 Issue 4, p77.

Horn Book Magazine Reviews. 2008. "The Seer of Shadows." Review of *The Seer of Shadows* by Avi. Horn Book Magazine, May/June 2008. http://www .thereadingwarehouse.com/book.php?ISBN=9780060000172

Horn Book Magazine Reviews. 2008. "The Eye of the Crow." Review of *The Eye of the Crow* by Shane Peacock. Horn Book magazine, Spring 2008.

Jeffers, Oliver. 2010. *The Heart and the Bottle*. New York: Philomel Books.

Lacombe, Benjamin. 2007. *Cherry and Olive*. New York: Walker.

McGee, Marni, and Ian Beck. 2006. *Winston the Book Wolf*. London: Bloomsbury Books.

Myers, Walter Dean. 2003. "Visit." In *Necessary Noise: Stories About Our Families as They Really Are*, edited by Michael Cart; illustrations by Charlotte Noruzi. New York: Joanna Cotler Books.

Patterson, James. 2005. *Maximum Ride: The Angel Experiment*. New York: Little, Brown and Company.

Paulsen, Gary. 1987. *Hatchet*. New York: Simon and Schuster.

Peacock, Shane. 2007. *The Eye of the Crow*. Toronto: Tundra Books.

Pilkey, Dav. 1996. *The Paperboy*. New York: Orchard Books.

Saricks, Joyce. 2005. *Readers' Advisory in the Public Library, Third Edition*. Chicago: ALA Editions.

Stewart, Trenton Lee. 2007. *The Mysterious Benedict Society.* New York: Little, Brown and Company.

Tarshis, Lauren. 2007. *Emma-Jean Lazarus Fell Out of a Tree.* New York: Penguin Group.

VandeVelde, Vivian. 2007. *Remembering Raquel.* Orlando: Harcourt Inc.

Viorst, Judith. 1990. *Earrings!* New York: Aladdin Paperbacks.

Vizzini, Ned. 2008. "Young and in the Way." Review of *Unwind,* by Neal Shusterman. New York Times, March 16, Sunday Book Review. http://www.nytimes.com/2008/03/16/books/review/Vizzini-t.html.

Watt, Melanie. 2006. *Scaredy Squirrel.* Tonawanda, New York: Kids Can Press.

Woodson, Jacqueline. 2004. *Coming on Home Soon.* New York: Putnam's

Index

Note: *denotes books best suited to teaching the particular appeal term.

About the Author

OLGA M. NESI is a library coordinator for the Office of Library Services in the New York City Department of Education. Prior to accepting this position in September 2011, she was the school librarian at Joseph B. Cavallaro I.S. 281 for eleven years. She received a BA in English from the State University of New York at Buffalo. Her Master of Library Science is from Queens College in Queens, New York, and she has a Master of Science in School Building Leadership from Mercy College in New York. Her article "It's All About Text Appeal" appeared in the August 2010 issue of *School Library Journal*. "A Vocabulary to Discuss Reading: Beyond 'Interesting'" appeared in the March 2012 issue of *School Library Monthly*. "The Transformative Power of Care" appeared in the May/June 2012 issue of *Knowledge Quest*.